NEVER THE
SAME AGAIN

Never the Same Again

Robert Simpson

Robert Simpson

HAMILTON & Co. Publishers
LONDON

CHAPTER ONE

On a lovely late summer morning I sat with my parents in the living room of our cottage deep in the Sussex countryside, awaiting the Prime Minister's broadcast, which when it came, informed us that we were at war with Germany. Mother said, "Oh dear! I have lived through one war and certainly didn't want another," to which father replied, "Well at least we now know where we stand." At the end of the broadcast I left the cottage and made my way through the gardens of the estate and out on to the path through the cricket field which led to the village. I was fifteen years old at the time and really knew very little about politics, but was convinced even then that it was going to be a long war. As I moved on towards the village to seek the company of friends I wondered how the coming days and weeks and years would affect this village in which I had been born and had grown up. As I reached the gate leading to the road an air raid warden came along on a bicycle shouting, "Air raid warning, red; take cover." I wondered then, as I turned for home, if anything would ever be the same again.

My father had been head gardener at a place near Canterbury, but the owner's wife was often the worse for drink, and father, having received conflicting orders on a number of occasions, decided the time had come to make a move. He applied for and obtained a post as head gardener to Mr Keith Rowlands, well known in the world of literature, who lived at a house called "Southcourt" in the village of Barnfield.

Father started work there two or three years after the first world war, got on well with Mr and Mrs Rowlands and enjoyed his work. The gardener's house at Southcourt was next door to the chauffeur's, and my brother and the chauffeur's son used to play quite happily together, but this situation did not last too long, owing, I gathered, to the fact that the chauffeur's mother who lived with him, often interfered with the two boys and various things were said which caused my mother some distress.

Things did not improve, and at the beginning of 1924, father, hearing of another job in the same village, made up his mind to leave Southcourt, and in March moved to Beechwood, owned by two maiden ladies. It was there, at Beechwood Cottage in May of the same year, that I was born.

Childhood

The past - it is a magic word
Too beautiful to last
It looks back like a lovely face
Who can forget the past?
There's music in its childhood
That's known in every tongue
Like the music of the wildwood
All chorus to the song.

The happy dream, the joyous play,
The life without a sigh,
The beauty thoughts can ne'er portray,
In those four letters lie.
The painter's beauty breathing art,
The poet's speaking pens
Can ne'er call back a thousandth part
Of what that word contains.

The finest summer sinks in shade,
The sweetest blossom dies,
And age finds every beauty fade
That youth esteemed a prize.
The play breaks up, the blossom dies,
And childhood disappears,
For higher dooms ambition tries
And care grows into years.

But time we often blame him wrong
That rude destroying time,
And follow him with sorrow's song
When he hath done no crime.
Our joys in youth are often sold
In folly's thoughtless fray,
And many feel their hearts grow old
Before their heads are grey.

The past, there lies in that one word
Joys more than wealth can crown,
Nor could a million call them back
Though muses wrote them down.
The sweetest joys imagined yet,
The beauties that surpast
The dearest joys man ever met
Are all among the past.

John Clare (1793-1864)

The village of Barnfield, some fifteen miles inland from the Sussex coast and roughly the same from the Kent border, has one main street running along a ridge situated between two valleys with various smaller roads leading off on either side. Beechwood was on the upper slope on the

3

southern side overlooking the River Dudwell Valley. The estate consisted of the house and gardens, a chauffeur's lodge and our cottage surrounded by four fields: Long Meadow to the east, Drive Field to the west, Seven Acres to the south and the cricket-field to the north. The drive to the big house naturally ran through Drive Field. Near to where it joined the main road in a corner of the cricket field stood the chauffeur's lodge. Our cottage was just to the north of Seven Acres, and separated from the main gardens on the north and east sides by dense thickets of laurel bushes and odd yew trees, with a path leading through them to the pleasure-grounds. On the western side we were separated by a twelve foot hawthorn hedge from Drive Field. The cottage was bordered by its own garden on three sides, which was about a quarter of an acre in extent.

The cottage, as I first remember it, had a fairly large living room and a rather larger sitting room with three bedrooms above. At the back was a very draughty scullery and a larder. A toilet of the bucket type was to be found as one of a range of three outbuildings beside Drive Field hedge. However, when I was four years old the two ladies, the elder of whom was known to us as Miss Barrington, and the other as Miss Emma, decided to demolish the back quarters of the house and some months later we had an indoor flush toilet, a large scullery containing a sink with a cold tap, a bath with cold water, and a huge copper with a fireplace under it in addition to an entry porch and a larder, which was about eight feet by six feet. The bath was fitted with a hinged lid which, when closed, provided a working surface. The living room was almost square with a solid fuel cooking range on one side, a huge cupboard under and a door leading to the staircase on another, with a window of small diamond panes as they all were on a third. The sitting room was also rectangular with the window facing south. It had walls covered with, and a ceiling of, square asbestos sheets with strips of grey painted wood covering the joints.

4

This was a delightful room, cool in summer and warm in winter, with a lovely view of the valley below and the rising ground on the far side of the river. Strangely enough the room had a small cellar, but as it meant lifting the floor covering to reach the trapdoor, it was never used. The big bedroom was occupied by my parents while my brother and I each had one of the smaller rooms, mine having two windows, one facing east and the other south.

Around the walls of the house were various plum trees, two of which never produced much fruit, but on the west side father planted a Victoria plum and a greengage, and many a feed my friends and I had from those two trees on late summer days. On the wall beneath and around my bedroom window was a pink rose (I never knew its name) with the most delightful scent. To wake in that room on smiling summer mornings with the sum streaming through the open window together with the perfume of that rose is something that will remain in my memory forever.

The garden itself contained one apple tree, a Norfolk Beefin, which produced just about the hardest cooking apples I've ever come across, as it seemed almost impossible to bruise them, and they were as good in March as when put into store in October; and a Rivers plum, the fruit of which was ripe in August. In one corner of the garden was a hen house and run, and a little wooden slide set in the hedge, which gave the chickens access to Seven Acres, where they became free-range hens and so produced eggs with deep yellow yolks of the type rarely seen nowadays from battery hens.

The rest of the garden was mainly planted with flowers. Besides his wages of £2.10s. (£2.50) a week, father had the cottage rent-free and £5 a year for milk plus any vegetables he wanted from the estate garden. Because our vegetables came from the estate we grew very little in this line except perhaps a few lettuces, radishes and spring onions which were close at hand when mother wanted them. Flowers were grown by both mother and father because they were both fond of flowers and also because they could be sold. We had all sorts which gave us blooms in the garden from early spring until late autumn, especially those which provided good cut flowers; daffodils by the hundred, polyanthus, tulips, lily of the valley, geums, lupins, pinks, delphiniums, gailardias, gypsophila, campanula, phlox, chrysanthemum maximum, pyrethrums, sweet peas, dahlias, chrysanthemums and michaelmas daisies. All these were to be found there, and many others. On Friday of each week mother would pick whatever was wanted, placing them in vases and jugs and then when father had finished his work he started putting the flowers into bunches for people who bought them each week, usually to put on graves of relatives. When they were all bunched I had the job of delivering these and I walked miles dropping off a 6d. (2½p) bunch at one house, and a 9d. one at another, then returning home to pick up others to take to houses lying in a different direction. This sale of flowers produced a few extra shillings each week, which used to provide the odd luxury such as a day at the seaside or some additional item of clothing.

On leaving the cottage by the path which wound its way between the laurel bushes, one suddenly came to an open space on the right which was at three different levels. The highest piece of ground was lawn with a number of mature trees including an arbutus or strawberry tree, and a tulip tree at the far end. On three sides the ground sloped down into what was also known as the iris garden, but I have no idea why, as during my childhood it was always planted with large groups of astilbes in red, pink and white. On the south side of the iris garden a few steps between poles led down to a larger, flat lawn, which was known as the tennis court, but I never recall tennis being played there. The

6

Barrington sisters and their guests frequently played croquet there in summer-time. The equipment for this was stored in a little shed in one corner. The path from the cottage continued north and soon after passing the steps leading down into the iris garden it divided in two directions. The one to the left ran westwards along the edge of the main lawn and pleasure-grounds in front of the big house. After passing a magnificent wellingtonia at the edge of the lawn, the path reached the entrance to a duck pen which was sited beside the Drive Field boundary. The path to the right ran between groups of rhododendrons and then turned left into the orchard. Beyond this was the main kitchen garden on either side of a path edged with box. Shrubs on one side separated this garden from the pleasure-grounds and on the other side a hawthorn hedge, almost twelve feet high, divided the garden from Long Meadow. At the top, a green door set in this hedge enabled one to reach the field. Near the door were the greenhouse, cold frames, fruit room and potting-shed. A laurel hedge separated this area from the drive at the end of which was a large wash and garage, and various store rooms for chicken food and cans of petrol. The petrol was for the generating plant which provided the big house with electricity. This was housed in an adjoining building. Across the drive was another large piece of ground, part of which was used for bedding with flowers and growing dahlias on either side of a grass path as well as a large herbaceous border. To the west of this and bordering the path to the cricket field were a few bush apples and the soft fruit cage. To the north, on the other side of a fence which supported blackberries and loganberries, was another kitchen garden where potatoes and green-stuff were usually grown.

Just outside the green door were some farm buildings where cattle, belonging to a farmer who rented Drive Field, Seven Acres and Long Meadow, were housed in winter time. To the south side of these buildings was a fenced yard where cattle could be penned. There was also a stack yard around which was a wire fence to prevent the cattle, when turned out, from eating the hay. To the north of this area was another smaller piece of ground where Miss Emma, who was a bit of a chicken fancier, kept her birds, although they were more often looked after by the garden staff. Miss Emma did do quite a lot of showing, and there were prize cards pinned up on the walls of the food room. I remember a Rhode Island Red cockerel that had won several prizes at various shows, becoming crop-bound, and it seemed that it would not survive. Father, in desperation, took it round to the potting-shed, knocked it out with the peak of his cap and proceeded to operate on the potting-bench. He opened the cockerel's neck with his budding-knife and emptied the bird's crop. He then obtained a needle and black cotton from home to sew up the incision. Much to his surprise I think, he found that the neck consisted of several layers of skin which he decided he could not separate, so they were bunched together and sewn up in one go. The cock recovered remarkably quickly and was in a matter of days moving around as though nothing had happened to it. I believe it subsequently won another prize.

From the green door an ash path which effectively split the field into two parts, ran across Long Meadow and through a beech plantation on the far side. A gate from this plantation led across the corner of an adjoining field to another gate which gave entry to a smaller field belonging to The Stag Hotel. After crossing this one reached the village street.

In comparison with many, Barnfield was I suppose, a large village and perhaps in some parts of the country it would have been regarded as a small town as it had a population of about two thousand. These inhabitants must have been thirsty souls, as the village had five public-houses as well as an off-licence. The Stag I have

8

mentioned, and there were also The Red Lion, Kings Head, Cross Keys and The Duke of Wellington. Nobody had to walk too far for a drink, as The Red Lion was at one end of the village street and The Duke of Wellington at the other, with the rest spaced at more or less equal distances in-between. Actually the Kings Head was down a short lane which led to the football field and the entrance to a farm. The Cross Keys was right opposite the village church, confirming the old rhyme -

> "Wherever God erects a house of prayer,
> The devil always builds a temple there."

The village was well supplied with shops, and when I was a child you could buy almost anything you were likely to need. There were five grocers' shops, two of which also sold drapery, clothing and furniture; two butchers', both of whom had some farmland and their own slaughter houses; two bakers'; two newsagents and stationers'; a fish shop; a chemist's; a fruiterer's and greengrocer's; a cycle shop; a saddler's; two tailors'; an ironmonger's; two coal merchants', one of whom also sold chicken food, garden sundries and second-hand furniture; two sweet shops and one of these also sold antiques; two boot repairers'; two garages; a wheelwright's with a cycle department attached; a barber and a post office. Like the public-houses these were all scattered along the main street, most of them being on the same side as the single pavement. At intervals there were pollarded lime trees planted at the edge of the pavement where it joined the road. These gave the village a very attractive appearance especially when they were in leaf in the summer time. Outside one of the baker's shops was a mounting block which had no doubt been there from the time when many of the people coming into the village from outlying farms had ridden in on horses. I never saw it used, but of course by the twenties and thirties most of the farmers, shopkeepers and people from the larger houses had motor transport. Besides the parish church of St Mark's, the village also boasted two chapels, a Methodist and a Baptist, all three of which were pretty well filled on Sundays, so I suppose in addition to being thirsty the parishioners were reasonably devout. As well as these places of worship, on the outskirts of the village to the north was St Mary's RC Church and to the south a C. of E. mission room. There was a school attached to St Mary's for the Roman Catholic children, but most of us went to the local C. of E. school, which was situated in what was officially Cross Keys Alley, but better known as School Lane. This turned off the main street opposite the Cross Keys and skirted the churchyard for fifty yards or so. Besides the school there was a scattering of dwelling-houses including one typical old Sussex farm house, the owners of which had their land at the other end of the village near The Turnpike. I never found any records of it or heard anything about it, but judging from the name there must have been a turnpike or toll gate there in days gone by. Near The Turnpike and opposite the drive gates of Beechwood was Brook Lane, which was bordered on one side by farmland and on the other by a nine hole golf course. At the bottom of Brook Lane was the brook and beyond it the road became Acland Hill. At the top of this the ground fell away to the north into the Rother Valley. Beyond The Turnpike on the main road, a lane - Southcourt Lane - led southward to Southcourt, which stood in the valley of the Dudwell River. Opposite the Duke of Wellington which was at The Green, was a side road called Wood Lane, which ran in a northerly direction and crossed the railway on the way to the next village. There was no station there but two small gates which could be used if you wanted to cross the line on foot. Beside the large gates across the road stood a gatekeeper's cottage, and if in a car, one stopped, sounded the horn and waited for the gatekeeper to emerge and open the gates in order that one might cross the line. I well remember one gatekeeper there who had twin daughters, and although they attended the

10

village school and I saw them most days, I never did learn to tell one from the other.

So this was the setting in which I spent my early days and although my friends and I did not have half the material possessions that children have today, I had a happy childhood and can look back on it today with much pleasure.

CHAPTER TWO

I don't know whether you have ever thought about your earliest memory, but mine remains quite vividly in my mind. It was a sunny, early summer morning and I know I was wearing a white blouse and white shorts. On going round the garden I found on the path beside the greengage plum tree, a small animal, apparently dead. I had seen mice and this appeared to be mouse-like, but somehow different. I went in search of father to tell him about my find. Father had a wide knowledge of country life and I learned much from him of natural history matters over the years. Having found father we went to look and my mouse-like creature turned out to be a bat. I was shown how the space between its limbs was covered with a membrane which formed its wings. Later I found out that it was a pipistrelle and of course over the years I saw bats flying on many occasions, and we had them coming through the bedroom windows at odd times, which used to put mother in a panic, as she was frightened that one of these creatures would become entangled in her hair. Father told her that this was not the case, but she never really believed him although he used to ask her how many ladies with long hair she had known who had had this sort of trouble with bats. She hadn't known any but nonetheless was still apprehensive. The bats, however, always passed out of the window through which they had entered without any damage being done. Of course I later learned that bats send out short-wave signals in the form of squeaks or pulses, the reflected echoes of which provide them with information on the position of surrounding objects and so enable them to avoid flying into things in the dark; and they also allow them to find their food of insects which fly at dark or in the twilight.

My next memory is of the rebuilding of the rear of our cottage. This was indeed excitement to a small boy. Several workmen arrived and the scullery and larder were demolished, new footings dug and the rebuilding started. Of course we had piles of sand, bags of cement, and stacks of bricks around the house, and a builder's shed in the garden, all of which provided interest for a small boy who had never had the opportunity to poke his nose into such things before. When the new scullery had been built, the bath, sink and copper were installed. This was followed by the fitting of the bowl in the toilet and of course the connection of the water. A trench was dug across the garden to Seven Acres and drainpipes were laid to a cesspool which was built in what to me seemed a huge hole just outside the garden gate. After the cement of the bottom and sides had been poured and had set I remember going down a ladder with a workman into the cesspool to view it from the inside. Every so often a little man, who seemed much smaller than my father - who was only five feet six inches tall - came to inspect the work. He had a little dark moustache and always wore a blue suit and a black bowler hat. I don't know why but mother didn't like him and always referred to him as "that bumptious little man".

The workman I liked most was a carpenter who brought me sweets telling me that he grew them in his allotment and had to mow them every so often. I was silly enough to believe him but sensible enough to ask him from time to time whether he had been mowing. He told me to call him George, which was a surprise, as I had never been permitted to call grown-ups anything but Mister, Mrs or Miss. I spent hours watching George work as he fitted door frames and doors, window frames and skirting board. He also, I

13

remember, glazed the windows and fitted sheets that he called beaver board to form the ceilings. I think George must have liked children, as he never seemed to mind my incessant chatter and endless questions. Although I must have got in his way on many occasions he never grumbled. The firm that did the building traded under the name of A.C. Startin and came from a village called Flimwell. I learned this much later when I could read, as the name was on the man-hole cover just below the toilet window. I was sorry when the builders went, as I had enjoyed having so much company and watching them at work. Mother, however, was pleased to see the back of them, as although she was glad to have the new rooms, she was tired of the mess and inconvenience. She was none too thrilled when within a few months one wall developed a huge crack, and the workmen had to return to build a buttress to stop the wall from falling down. Seeing he had been inspecting the work as it progressed in the first place, the bumptious little man came in for a fair amount of criticism from mother.

Once the building was completed, bath-night became great fun. Previously we had bathed in a galvanised zinc bath, but now there was a gleaming white enamel bath with a cold tap. I don't suppose this arrangement would be very popular today, but to produce the hot water, the copper had to be lit. Friday night was bath-night. After the flowers had all been bunched and delivered, mother used to clear up the buckets, vases, bits of stalk and stripped leaves, while father went off to bring in pieces of wood from one of the sheds in the garden. In one corner of the garden was a wood-pile which came from dangerous boughs of trees on the estate and which had been sawn off from prunings. On occasions, a tree was felled for some reason or another, and wood that was no use for timber found its way on to the pile. Near the pile was a sawing horse and a chopping block. When he found time father sawed or chopped wood which was then stored in the shed to keep it dry. When the wood was brought in, the copper fire was lit. This fire not only heated the water but also warmed the room. When the water was hot enough it had to be taken from the copper by bucket and tipped into the bath. The copper then had to be refilled with cold water, again by buckets filled from the tap over the sink, and the fire stoked ready for the next person to bathe. The following morning all the wood left over had to be collected up and returned to the shed, then the ashes from the copper fire had to be raked out and put in a bucket for transfer to the garden where it was eventually dug in. The linoleum-covered floor had then to be washed over and dried. All this I suppose took over an hour, so really bath-night with its preparations and cleaning up afterwards was a major operation.

When I was small, the chauffeur was a man called Colin East, who lived with his wife and children in The Lodge. I never really knew much about them and some months before I started school he left and the family moved away. He was replaced by a Mr Kenward, who had a girl of about nine, and a boy, Bert, who was a month older than me. Soon after they moved in I went over to The Lodge to ask if he could come out to play. He could and did and we became firm friends and did all sorts of things together in the following years until we joined the Forces in 1942 and went our separate ways.

The Kenwards had come from Dallington, and Bert had already been to school for a little while there but we both started at Barnfield School at the beginning of the summer term of 1929. The head teacher at that time was a Mr Read, who I believe retired at the end of my first term. I only remember seeing him once and really didn't know who he was at the time, but found out later from my brother, who is seven and a half years older than me and who had been familiar with Mr Read for some years. I gather Mr Read didn't spend much of his time with the infants, where of course I started. In fairness he had his own class to teach, Standard V11, where those about to leave school were to be found. Non-teaching heads in village schools were at that time almost unknown. Mr Read was replaced by the new head, Mr Atkins, who was there for the rest of my time at the school. Mrs Heath was the infant teacher who had been at the school for some years and was there for some years after I had left. I can't remember too much about my time in the infants, but I found Mrs Heath was very pleasant but expected us to do exactly as we were told. As I was used to doing as I was told at home, this came as no great hardship and was only what I had expected. She let Bert and me sit together because we were friends, but she insisted on calling me Bobby, which I didn't like but could do nothing about. At home I was always called plain Bob, and that was the way I liked it and still do.

I remember learning to read, which with a bit of help from my brother at home, I didn't find too difficult. Letters and figures were not at first written on paper or in exercise books, but with chalk on a small black-surfaced board made of thick cardboard. We each, I remember, had to provide a duster to clean these boards. When we were told "Clean your boards, children," there was vigorous polishing of the boards, and chalk dust flew in all directions. Of course we soon discovered that the more one polished the bigger dust-storm was created, so we did our best on every possible occasion. Pictures in those days in school rooms were, if our school was anything to go by, few and far between. We had one picture frame into which were put four pictures, one at a time, for each season of the year. I can only really remember the picture of spring, which was of a cherry orchard in full bloom, with sheep and lambs in the grass below the trees.

The room in which we were taught was not particularly attractive, having a very high ceiling, and although there were several windows, the sills were very high and we could not look out through the windows. Looking back I feel that perhaps the designers sighted the windows deliberately in this way to prevent pupils being distracted from the lessons by gazing at the scene outside. The walls were painted a dark green. Round the lower part of the room was a dado some two and a half feet high, made of wood and painted a dark brown. Mrs Heath did her best to brighten the room by placing flowers and leaves in containers on the window sills. Vases were not provided in those days and most of the containers were jam jars. Seeing father was a gardener, I used to take flowers from time to time to help to keep the containers filled.

Around the dado were placed at intervals posters showing the upper and lower case letters, and bearing pictures of items, the initial letter of which began with the particular letter shown. We also had similar posters showing figures. After the one came a picture of one egg; after the two a couple of apples were illustrated and so on to the figure nine.

In the centre on one side of the room was a coal burning stove beside which stood a large scuttle filled with coal. At morning break and at dinnertime an older boy from one of the top classes came round to re-stoke the stove. If you happened to sit somewhere near the stove you were nice and warm, but if you sat at either end of the room, not much heat was forthcoming during the winter months. All the classrooms were heated in the same way. During my time there I sat about as far away from the stove as it was possible to do. At a later date I became one of the stokers, and found this rather annoying having to stoke up the fire for the benefit of those who sat near it while I retired to the furthest corner of the room. There was no chance of getting nearer the fire at break-time either, as apart from wet days we were always despatched to the playground at these times. As infants we shared the girls' playground, as it had been decided, I suppose, that the older girls would be more gentle with us than the older boys. When after two years the boys among us graduated to the "large" playground, I saw the point of this.

In one corner of the infant room was a door leading to a cloakroom which we shared with the older girls. This was a cold, damp, miserable place with a framework in the centre attached to which were coat hooks. Along the side were a few chipped, once-upon-a-time white, washbasins with cold taps only. At the end of the row was a fitment with a roller towel, which it seemed to me had to last us the whole week. As everybody used it, it was wet within half an hour of its being placed there, and remained wet until it was taken away for washing. The days of hot water, liquid soap and paper towels were some way off. This cloakroom also served as a waiting room when the school doctor came to carry out his examinations.

The afternoon session used to begin at 1.30 p.m. during most of the year, but during the darkest days of winter we started at 1.15 p.m. so that we could finish a quarter of an hour earlier in order to give those who had a long way to walk the chance to get a good part of the way home before it became quite dark. I well recall one occasion when the times were changed, walking into the classroom just before half past one only to find that everyone else was already at work. Yes, of course although I had been told of the change, I had forgotten.

The children remained in the infant room for two years, then were transferred to another room in which standards one and two were taught. This was a more pleasant room with a big window facing south; consequently on sunny days the room was bright and cheerful. Here I remember learning about Greeks and Romans, and also about

Eskimos, Red Indians and Africans. In fact we had a text book called "Children of Other Lands". This to me was very interesting, as books at home were strictly limited and the local library boxes which were housed in the village institute didn't offer too much for children, and of course there was no television. At that time we didn't have a wireless set at home. It was in one of these classes that we first started using ink. Each desk had two inkwells, one for each child. These were presumably filled by the caretaker. There was, however, a can with a long spout which was left in the room. This was used for topping-up operations when necessary. We each had a dip pen. At first one did not put enough ink on the nib, and so after the first stroke or so it refused to write, or one put too much on, which gave you enough ink to write with and usually produced a blot from the excess. We all had a sheet of pink blotting paper which rapidly turned blue as we made constant use of it. Surprisingly, in a short time, most of us learned the right amount of ink required and we started to produce pages of written work without blotty decorations. Perhaps the ruler which landed across your knuckles from time to time after a particularly messy effort helped to make you progress more quickly.

These two classes were taught in my time by a young woman with auburn hair who was named Miss Perkins. On the whole I have quite happy memories of her, as she was usually a fairly gentle soul who introduced us to all sorts of interesting things. I can remember clearly the jam jars containing pink blotting paper, kept damp, and germinating peas and beans showing between the paper and the glass. We spent two years in this room before moving up to what we called Standard Three. Miss Perkins left the school soon after I had moved on and went, I believe, to Africa to work for a missionary society.

The next two years were spent with a Mrs Scott in what

was, I suppose, the largest and dullest classroom in the school. The windows were on the north side so the room received no direct sunlight and I cannot remember any windows on the south side, as the headmaster's house was attached to this wall. To the east was the classroom we had just left and to the west was a large movable partition which separated this classroom from the one next door. It could be opened to make the two rooms into one. This was done each morning for assembly when we had hymn singing and prayers followed by any announcement Mr Atkins wished to make. For the rest of the day the partition was closed, and access to the next room was through a small door set in one section of the partition. The two classes in this room, standards three and four, were taught by Mrs Scott who I believe was a native of Barnfield and who spent her entire teaching career at the village school. Including her days as a pupil I suppose she had been there for over forty years when I moved into her class. Apart from arithmetic which I enjoyed with her I have no very clear memories of the things we did in her classes and no particular feelings about her. I neither liked her very much nor disliked her. Having mixed with and taught several generations of Barnfield children she obviously knew some of the families of the village extremely well and was in the habit of saying to a pupil with whom she was displeased, "You're a (name of family) to the backbone." I was told on various occasions that I was a Simpson to the backbone, although she knew a good deal less about our family than some, however she had taught my brother. I was always quite pleased with the remark, although it was meant to be disparaging, as I was quite proud of being a Simpson. I remember Mrs Scott's husband, who was a very cheerful man and a carpenter by trade. He was secretly known to us children as Lobby Ludd. It was about this time that one of the daily papers had a promotion campaign at seaside resorts during the holiday season. Posters were put up in various places stating where Lobby Ludd would be on certain days, and If you could recognise him and show him a copy of the particular paper concerned (I've forgotten which one it was now) you could claim a cash prize. You had to walk up to the man after recognising him and say something like, "You are Lobby Ludd. I am carrying a copy of the Daily - and claim my cash prize." Of course the inevitable happened and many people were wrongly recognised as Lobby Ludd. I gather that Mr Scott was in Hastings one day during this time and someone approached him with, "You're Lobby Ludd....." Of course he told one or two people, therefore the news soon got around the village. On hearing this we children thought it hilarious and ever after he was known to us by this name. Mind, one had to be careful on meeting him in the village to remember to say, "Good morning, Mr Scott," and not, "Good morning, Lobby Ludd." I suppose it was the sound of the name which amused us so much.

After two years with Mrs Scott we moved on to the next room which housed standards five and six which were taught by a young man who had come to the school the year before. His name was Mr Turner and I hit it off with him from the beginning. I very much enjoyed my two years with him. He was extremely strict and few people stepped out of line when he was around. He demanded good behaviour and insisted that we did as much work as we were capable of, and that to the best of our ability. He seemed to set much higher standards than we had previously been used to and this I believe did us all good. I always found him completely fair. It was a case of you did what he asked and enjoyed the work or you did less than you were capable of and suffered for it. To us boys he was something of a hero in any case, as he played for the village football team and seemed to score goals week after week. At a later date I believe there was a disagreement and he went off to play for Eastbourne who played in a league where standards were higher.

During my second year with Mr Turner, a school event took place which has remained vividly in my mind ever since. Mr Atkins the head, decided to arrange a day's outing to London for children in the top two classes. In these present times an outing to London may seem a very small event, but to children of the working classes in the nineteen-thirties it was something to be eagerly looked forward to and to be remembered long afterwards. Few of us in the group, including me, had ever been to London and it therefore seemed a marvellous opportunity to see some of the things and places we had heard about. I remember considerable preparation being done for this outing. We were all given a notebook in which we wrote down the stations through which we would pass on the way to London, and information about the places to be visited. I retained that notebook for years after. Strangely enough I cannot now recall how we got to the station, which was some three miles away, but get there we did, and then enjoyed a two hour rail journey to Charing Cross. Where did we go in London? We visited Trafalgar Square with its monument to Nelson, the four great lions at the base of the column, and the fountains. It was an interesting surprise to find on one side of the square, set in cement, the imperial measures of length.

After leaving Trafalgar Square we walked down the Mall past the Duke of York Column, and on to Buckingham Palace. Later we saw the Cenotaph and were shown the various government offices, at that time to be found in Whitehall. We marched into Downing Street where we stood and gazed at Number Ten, where Stanley Baldwin was the occupant, but the only person we saw was the proverbial policeman on duty at the door. We toured Westminster Abbey with its tombs of former monarchs, its Poets' Corner and the tomb of the unknown warrior. From there we walked The Strand and Fleet Street, gazing at the offices of national newspapers, and eventually to St Paul's

Cathedral, which we explored from Nelson's tomb in the crypt to the great cross on the dome.

After that came a visit to the Tower of London, with its Traitors' Gate, Tower Green, St John's Chapel and the ravens. Inside the White Tower we saw the weapons we had previously only heard about in our history lessons and we viewed with considerable interest the suits of armour and other items from wars of long ago. On then we went to see the crown jewels at which we gazed in wonder, having never seen anything like them before. We didn't even have to take our lunch, but ate in a restaurant. Was it Lyons, or the Tower Restaurant? I cannot be sure, but to eat out was to us an event in itself. I do know that I managed to get fish, as in those days I was not very keen on meat.

On our return to Charing Cross we saw the Monument erected to commemorate the Great Fire of London. We felt that at least we now knew something of the famous London buildings, as in addition to our tours we had seen the Bank of England, Tower Bridge and the Embankment, and now we knew where St Martin's in the Fields was to be found, and what the National Gallery looked like from the outside.

We had much to talk about on the journey home and for days afterwards. I have always been grateful to Mr Atkins for arranging that outing, and although I have since re-visited all those places and examined them in greater detail, the pleasure derived from those first visits has remained with me down the years.

Another event which comes to mind from my school days was the annual gathering round the war memorial on Armistice Day. The memorial stands in the middle of the road at the beginning of School Lane, opposite The Cross Keys and near the church. We used to march in twos in a long crocodile up the hill to the memorial. There we stood class by class while the vicar conducted a service in memory of the fallen whose names were inscribed on the sides of the memorial. We were told before we went, that during the two minutes silence we should thank God that there had been such men who had given their lives for the freedom of Britain. This was difficult for us really, as although there were many names on that memorial for a village the size of Barnfield, and we knew that these men had been killed, we had not known them personally, nor could we really visualise then the horror of the battlefields of France and Flanders. We were a different generation. Our fathers, although many had fought in the war, were still alive and I'm afraid that to us, the men who had fallen in the Battle of the Somme were no more real than those who had perished at Waterloo or Trafalgar. I know that we always sang "Oh God our help in ages past", and I can still recall all the words without referring to a hymn book...Perhaps to us the difficult verse to understand was:

Time like an ever rolling stream,
Bears all its sons away,
They fly forgotten as a dream
Dies at the opening day.

After all it was very obvious that these men had not been forgotten and were not likely to be forgotten in the foreseeable future. Besides the memorial and the armistice service we were constantly reminded of them by a row of wooden crosses hanging in the church porch which had originally marked the graves of a dozen or so near the battlefields where they had been killed. These crosses had been brought back to the village at the end of the war when the war cemeteries were being established. Little did we realise then that in a few years the whole thing would start all over again, and that long before the end, we too should be involved in various ways.

The upper classes at school were at times involved in dancing round the maypole, which was set up in one of the playgrounds. Some children liked it, but it was not my cup of tea, as, not being musical I found I could make a mess of it without really trying. The girls I think, were keener than the boys, but as it didn't go particularly well it gradually faded from the curriculum. We certainly never danced on May Day, and as far as I can remember, nothing much did happen on May Day at our school as it was not then a national holiday, and was regarded as more or less a normal working day. We certainly went to school, and our way of marking the occasion was to wear a sprig of hawthorn or May blossom. If you failed to do this, your toes were trodden on by anyone who had a sprig of May in their buttonhole. As most of we boys wore boots with nailed and plated heels and soles, our chief reason for wearing May was to avoid having our toes painfully flattened. In some years this could be decidedly difficult if Spring was late and May blossom was hard to come by. Those who managed to find some were definitely the winners.

Of course, in the upper part of the school, we played games. The boys played cricket in summer and football in winter, while the girls played stoolball and netball. From time to time matches were arranged against other schools, and if away from home, we usually travelled by bicycle, although on occasions we went by car, usually the headmaster's or perhaps one or two owned by helpful villagers. It was not difficult to pack eleven schoolboys into two or three cars. You didn't have to be very good to make the school team as numbers were such that only two or three boys had to be left out. I enjoyed playing football, but was never very good at it. Cricket was my real interest and even if I wasn't over talented at that, I played the game with real pleasure. I can clearly remember being asked by Mr Turner after dropping a catch whether I would like to borrow a bucket, and replying whilst rubbing my finger ends, "No thank you, sir." I think he was disappointed with the reply but probably pleased that my fingers were tingling.

Despite episodes of this nature I was always pleased to get on to a cricket field whenever the opportunity presented itself. After all, there have been others who have dropped catches over the years. Years later my keenness for cricket caught up with me. In 1943 I was in a transit camp in Mombassa waiting to join a ship to take me further east. One day after lunch I was lying on my bed reading, when a chief petty officer came into the hut and shouted, "Any of you fellows interested in cricket?" "Yes chief," I called, as I tumbled off the bed. "Good," he replied, "you can go to help roll the wicket for the officers' match." I might have known; I'd been told never to volunteer for anything.

Another subject popular with most of the boys, taught in the upper part of the school, was gardening. Sloping to the south beyond the girls' playground was a piece of land divided into garden plots, six if I remember correctly, for groups of boys to work on, with a seventh plot at the bottom which was planted with fruit. Each plot was worked by five or six boys. Vegetable crops such as carrots, parsnips, swedes, turnips, peas, beans and cabbages were grown. At the end of the season when the crops were harvested, some of the produce was shared out among the boys, although I never got any as I suppose it was thought that my taking vegetables home would be like carrying coals to Newcastle. I did on occasions take cabbage plants and various other members of the brassica family to school for planting, as father always seemed to have a surplus, and was always willing to give stuff away to people who required it. In days when the weather was too bad to work outside we used to have gardening lessons in the classroom, which I liked better than working on the plots. I was interested in how things were grown but could never work up much enthusiasm for actually growing them. Mother used to say it was because I didn't like getting my hands dirty. At that time she was probably right. Although my father, grandfather and great grandfather, and probably my more ancient ancestors had all been gardeners, and my brother, too, by this time was working as a gardener, I never wished to earn my living in this way. Later on when I came to enjoy gardening as a hobby I preferred working in a greenhouse more than outside. This is still true today. The trouble at school was that because father was a gardener I was expected to be extremely keen at working on the plots. I still have a school report to prove the point, which says, "Written work - 60/64," and referring to the practical work, "Might work harder." Alas, it remained "might" as I never did work harder in the school gardens. I was hoeing in-between where carrots had been sown once, when not really looking what I was doing I hoed through the actual row. Another lad said to me, "You won't half catch it when Mr Atkins finds out." Seeing the carrots hadn't then germinated I was bright enough to reply, "Well, he won't know why they haven't come up unless you tell him, and if he does find out I shall know who told him." This bit of logic must have been sufficient, as I never heard anything more about the matter from the boys or Mr Atkins.

By this time I had decided that I would like to do clerical work, and mother and father decided that I should go on to a secondary school in order to give me a greater chance of achieving my aim. So at thirteen I left the village school, and went to school in Tonbridge. This, I might say, I have always been grateful for, as it was only personal sacrifices on the part of my parents that enabled me to go at all, as apart from school fees, there were my train season tickets to be paid for, and in the first place, a new bicycle for me to travel to and from the station.

CHAPTER THREE

Like any other schoolboy since schools began, I looked forward to weekends and holidays when I was free to do the things I wanted to do. Most of this leisure time was spent in the company of Bert Kenward. For most of the time we got on well and enjoyed each other's company. Occasionally, like most children, we fell out, but the periods of ignoring each other were usually short, and we soon took up where we had left off.

Of course in the early days we didn't go far away from Beechwood; in fact most of the time we spent in the cricket field, as apart from the cricket pitch there was a part of the field which we could use for anything we wanted to do. Sheep grazed there in winter time, but apart from that no animals were kept in the field. We couldn't go into Long Meadow or Seven Acres in spring and early summer because the grass was needed for hay-making, and we were not allowed to tread it down. The Drive Field usually had a milking herd in it, and the cows went into Long Meadow and Seven Acres after hay-making was over to graze the new growth of grass. We were not encouraged by the local farmer who hired the fields to play in them when the cows were out so we kept mainly to the cricket field.

A worn track ran across the lower part of the field where Bert's father walked each day from his cottage to the garage where the Barringtons' car was kept. Apart from driving he had other duties to do on the estate, such as running the engine which provided the big house with electric light, cleaning shoes in the big house, washing, polishing and other work on the car, and I believe he also looked after the Barringtons' dog, which had a kennel in a corner of the concreted area, usually known as the wash, just outside the garage. Some mornings he went to work wearing clothes which were suitable for doing these jobs, then if the car was wanted in mid-morning he would go home to change into his chauffeur's uniform. Of course he also went home to lunch, so over the years quite a pronounced track was formed. When it became muddy in winter a bucketful or two of ashes was put down here and there in the worst places, so this was the way anyone going from the house or gardens to the chauffeur's lodge went.

Above the path to the north was quite a steep bank, at the top of which the ground levelled out. Here the cricket pitch was situated. This bank had several bare patches where grass never grew to any great extent and it was here, when we were small, that Bert and I often played. In winter we often made mud pies. We collected a number of tins of various shapes and sizes including some old baking tins, and these we packed with muddy earth. Of course when turned out, the mud retained the shape of the tin. When we had made our stock we then played shops and sold our "pies" to each other.

This bank also provided fun in summer because when it was dry we enjoyed ourselves by rolling from the cricket pitch to the path. One could go down it in several ways; in a succession of backward rolls, or forward rolls, or just turning over from side to side.

On the other side of the cricket field, just above the main road and just outside the front garden of The Lodge was a sand-pit. Here we spent many happy hours digging sand and playing with it in much the same way as children do today. As this sand-pit overlooked the road, sometimes, when we were a little older and had learned to write with a fair degree of facility, we sat at the top taking down motor car registration numbers. Traffic in those days was such that we didn't miss many because in busier periods I would attend to the westbound traffic and Bert would record those going towards the village. Later we got hold of an old AA book and from the information contained in it we could find which cars were registered in the county and which came from outside. We learned quite a lot about registration numbers from different areas, and I can still recall that PN, PM and NJ were East Sussex registration letters. I suppose they eventually ran out of numbers to follow these letters because we saw plates beginning ANJ. Whilst doing this we often saw the AA man going past on his motor cycle with box-type sidecar in which his tools and equipment were carried. All motorists displaying an AA badge in those days received a salute from the AA patrol man, and we too were often acknowledged in the same way, without paying an AA subscription.

One summer's morning when Bert and I were playing in the sand, we were much surprised to see a number of soldiers come marching down the road, going in the direction of Brighton. These were followed at intervals by lorries with more soldiers in the back, guns, bren gun carriers, tanks and more marching soldiers. We soon packed up playing with the sand and stood by the railings, waving to each group as they passed. Soldiers seemed to like children, as we received waves and various shouts throughout the day. Yes, throughout the day they came and made their way along the road, all going in the same direction. What a sight it was for us boys, and very exciting too, as half of the things that passed we had never seen before. There was a certain number mounted on horses, and there were even mobile kitchens with chimneys smoking away, and steam coming from various containers attended by what were obviously army cooks. We watched all that day. Much to our surprise still more soldiers and equipment passed through the following morning. Of course there were gaps in the stream, and we kept thinking that we had seen the last when suddenly another group of vehicles or squads of marching soldiers came into view. I suppose they must have been taking part in manoeuvres. We never really knew what they were doing or where exactly they were going, but until then we never realised how many soldiers and vehicles there were. We obviously only saw a small part of the army, but to us at that age there seemed to be really thousands of troops moving through the village, and judging by the time they took to go through, there probably was quite a large number of men involved.

We had our own weapons too, as at Beechwood there were several good yew trees, and as all schoolboys knew, yew trees meant bows. We used to get one of my father's assistants, Harry Loader, or anyone else that cared to listen to us, to cut a few suitable lengths of yew for us to make into bows. We used to cut a groove at either end, tie a piece of string to one groove, then bend the bow and secure the free end of the string to the other groove. The arrows were made of straight pieces of thin ash or hazel between two and three feet long. We used to point them at one end and cut a groove at the other into which we fitted the string when we bent the bow. We were then ready for action as we never bothered about fitting flights to the arrows. We used to shoot at tin cans which we sometimes hit, and on occasions at sparrows which we always missed. If there were several of us playing, we sometimes had mad moments as we picked sides and then used to shoot at each other. We had been warned against this as it was very dangerous, especially to eyesight, but as boys we didn't see the danger and had our battles. Fortunately nobody ever seemed to get hurt in these encounters. At one time when I was quite small, my brother and his friends were

31

experimenting with arrows made of bamboo canes with the sawn-off shank of a skewer inserted in the end. I am not now sure whether it was one of these arrows or one of the other sort which he loosed off on one occasion when I was enthroned in the toilet. The arrow came in through the window and the point struck me in the forehead. I suppose it didn't really do very much damage but I was very young at the time and it frightened me as much as hurt me, but it was too close to my eyes for comfort. My father, who was normally a very placid man, really lost his temper over this episode, and my brother was suitably admonished with a leather strap, if I remember correctly. That incident put paid to bows and arrows for quite some time.

We sometimes went fishing either in one or other of the farm ponds or in the River Dudwell. I had a fishing rod, quite a good one really, which had belonged to my grandfather. It wasn't really my cup of tea but I went along with the other lads. If we went to one of the ponds we usually managed to catch carp, but no one wanted to eat them so we took the hook out and threw them back into the pond. Whether it caused the fish pain or not I'm still not sure, as this I understand is debatable, but it all seemed a bit pointless to me even in those days. I preferred the river fishing to the ponds, but here again one caught sticklebacks and minnows, which had to be put back. You were supposed to be able to catch trout, but I never managed to hook one, although I know that some of the men who went fishing caught them. Perhaps I was a poor fisherman or not sufficiently interested. I did, however, manage one day to catch two eels which I proudly took home. When I arrived, mother soon told me that she had never tried eels, but she certainly didn't fancy them as they looked too much like snakes, and she was frightened of snakes. Later, father had a look at them and said, "I don't think we'll bother. I'm not keen on eels as they taste earthy." Whether they did or not I'm still not sure as I have never tried them. Anyway, seeing my parents didn't want the eels, I put them out for the cat. When Sooty arrived home she soon approached them because cats are naturally nosey, and these were something new to her. After smelling around them for a minute or two she tossed both her head and her tail in the air and walked away. It seemed that nobody or nothing wanted my eels, so I took them round the garden, dug a hole and buried them. I suppose some plants benefited from the fish manure, but it seemed a bit of a waste and I wished I'd left them in the river. After all, they had swum across the Atlantic Ocean only to end in being buried in our garden. I think this more or less put me off fishing. I was always rather bored sitting around on the bank of a pond or river waiting, just waiting for a fish to bite, when there were many other things that I could have been doing. Strangely enough I later lived in Redditch, home of the fishing tackle industry, where every other man was a keen fisherman, and later in Leighton Buzzard where dozens of people fish in the Grand Union Canal, but I was never tempted. I could never raise enough enthusiasm to fish as an adult.

In winter time Bert and I, and some of our school friends, played football on a flat patch of ground between Bert's garden gate and the cricket pitch. Bert was quite useful as a goal-keeper. He stood on his line between the two coats we used to put down while the rest of us tackled each other and every so often blazed a shot in the direction of the "goal". Bert got plenty of exercise fetching the balls which went wide. Later we got hold of an old broom handle, sawed it in half and used the two pieces as goal posts. These football games went on on Saturday mornings, and during the Christmas holidays whenever the weather permitted. Heavy rain sometimes deterred us but I do not remember worrying much about the cold.

In summer we used the same strip for cricket. Sometimes when the men brought a horse to pull the big roller over the cricket pitch, they rolled our piece to flatten it a bit after the winter's football. Actually, they never minded our hitting balls across the pitch and subsequently retrieving them, as long as we kept off the cricket table. Sometimes the practice nets were left up at one side of the field, and in daytime we often used those. Some of the cricketers didn't approve if they saw us and would clear us off, but others tried to interest us in the game and didn't mind. Eventually a junior club was formed. We could join on paying a subscription of, I think, one and sixpence (seven and a half pence) a year.

Of course all children need heroes and ours were the men of the county side who at that time we had heard about and read about but never seen. As we played we took it in turn to be John or James Langridge, who appeared in the papers as Langridge John, and Langridge Jas; Jim or Harry Parks; Ted Bowley; Wally Cornford, who came from the nearby village of Hurst Green and kept wicket for the county; Bert Wensley; the Indian K.S. Duleepsinhji; or Maurice Tate, who we all knew had taken thirty-eight Australian wickets on the tour of 1924-25 when England had still lost by four matches to one, but he got another seventeen on the next tour of 1928-29 and that time England won by four matches to one. Eight times Maurice performed the cricketer's double of a thousand runs and a hundred wickets in a season. I, for one, thought he was marvellous. Unfortunately by the time I was able to see county cricket fairly regularly, Tate's career was over. He later became the landlord of a public house in the village of Wadhurst not so very far away.

In term time various other activities took place. There seemed to be seasons for different types, and these appeared to change from one to the other without any real pattern. Marbles in those days were as popular as they are in schools today. If my memory serves me correctly we used to buy fifty marbles of the clay variety for twopence of the old money. Usually a small hole was made almost anywhere where we were playing, and a marble was thrown on the ground by each of the two contestants, then flicked with the index finger towards the hole. The first person to get his marble into the hole collected his marble and that of his opponent. Another variation was the marble board which was a rectangular piece of wood with half circles cut out of the bottom, usually six in number. Each hole had a number painted over it, one to six. The idea was to hold the board vertically while facing your opponent and he, from a given distance, would roll a marble towards the board with the intention of getting it through one of the holes. If he failed, you collected his marble. If his marble entered a hole you paid out the number of marbles painted over the hole. I well remember the arguments we had at times as to which hole a marble had passed through, especially when numbers one and six were next door to each other. You definitely saw a marble roll through the hole marked one, and your "friend" claimed it had gone through the hole marked six, or if it had gone through the six hole you shouted that it was only one. Sometimes when a boy was not having much luck at getting a marble through a hole he accused the holder of the board of moving it at the crucial moment and got his friends to back up his opinion. I suppose we had as much fun arguing about it as we did playing the game, as it wasn't really often we accused each other of real cheating, and usually things were settled amicably between us.

Of course playing conkers was restricted to the period when they were available, and as we had hop-picking holidays in the summer time, and didn't start the autumn term until early October, it was usually at that time that we played. Living in the country meant that there was no great difficulty in obtaining conkers. Having obtained a stock of conkers, one bored a hole through each with an old nail, then choosing what looked a good one, threaded a string with a big knot at one end through the hole in the conker. You then found an opponent, and while one boy dangled his conker on its string, the other would swing his own and take an almighty swipe at his opponent's conker with the intention of hitting and breaking it. Roles were then reversed, and the game went on until one of the conkers was broken. If the conkers were being used for the first time the winner became known as a oncer and this went on until it was eventually broken. If a conker had broken say seven others it would be known as a sevener; if it then broke another which had previously broken five others it would become a thirteener. It was surprising how many conkers were credited with breaking large numbers. I am sure we added to the numbers at times for kudos purposes. Various methods were tried, like leaving conkers in the sun or baking them in the oven to make them harder. I did discover that the fruits of the white-flowered chestnut were a good deal harder than those of the pink or red-flowered variety. We had a red-flowered chestnut on the estate, and it was easy to collect conkers from it without much effort, but they were never successful, usually disintegrating at the first well struck blow.

Hoops were often a favourite in winter time because I suppose they gave us reason to run about and keep warm. There were, of course, no plastic hoops in those days, and few wooden ones. The wooden ones I remember were usually owned by girls whereas we boys had hoops made of iron. To bowl them along we had a piece of wood about two feet long through which was driven a nail at right angles. Once the hoop had been bowled with the hands and started turning, it could be kept going quite easily by pressing the nail against it and by pushing with the stick. It was surprising how adept some lads became at turning corners, doing figures of eight and various other movements without losing control. I have seen many a rusty hoop with a polished "silver" band on the outside where the nail rubbed against it as it turned. Just west of the Red Lion on the opposite side of the road stood the village institute which was used for the occasional concert, dance or other village social event. It also had a billiard room for the men of the village. I well remember coming home from school one afternoon with another friend, Ken Edwards, and having bowled our hoops the length of the village street we came to a stop by the gate of the farm where he lived, which was opposite the institute, or more or less so. Now at this time outside the institute was a hole in the road with a barrier around it, and as holes in roads have always attracted boys we crossed to see what was going on. Down in the hole were two men with picks and shovels. We stood there watching in order to find out what they were doing. After we had been there for some few minutes one of the men enquired, "What do you want?" to which I replied, "Nothing." He then said, "Have you got it?" I must admit, being ten or eleven I was somewhat mystified by the question, but as he obviously expected an answer I finally said rather hesitantly, "Yes." He then glared at Ken and me and bellowed, "Well now you've got it, bugger off." We were not really used to language of that sort in those days but we got the message and "buggered" off.

Tops were a favourite pastime at various times of the year. They came in a number of shapes and sizes. We had carrot tops which were shaped like a stump-rooted carrot, peg tops with a long steel spike at the bottom, and another which was called a window breaker. We had a piece of stick about two feet long to which was attached about a yard of string similar to that used in grocers' shops at that time. The string was wound tightly round the top, the base of the top was then placed in contact with the ground, and a sharp tug on the string set the top spinning rapidly. By lashing the top with the string it was fairly easy to keep it spinning and move it in the direction one wanted to go. Mind, some types of top were very much easier to manage than others. I cannot now recall the shape of the window breaker, but the idea was to lash the top with string, which would propel it through the air and it would continue spinning when it returned to the ground. This was much more difficult than driving the carrot top and was usually tried well away from windows, as breaking windows in my school days was not encouraged. I am sure there would have been considerable trouble at home had the glass in a shop window been broken and my parents had been asked to pay for it, as I am sure they would have been.

When Bert and I reached the age of about eleven, we both were lucky enough to acquire a bicycle each. Bert was the first to have one and I suppose my parents were reluctant to see me without. Anyway, father went off to the wheelwright's, whose son had a bicycle business and came home with a "White Heather", which in those days cost the princely sum of five shillings (twenty-five pence). Mind, five shillings took a bit of finding, as there was never as much as that left out of any one week's wages. I had a bit of trouble learning to ride a bicycle, as balancing and steering it in the right direction did not come easily to me. After considerable help from father I found on one occasion I was moving along the drive chattering to him but not getting any replies. I realised I was on my own and father no longer holding on to the rear of the saddle, whereupon I promptly fell off. It wasn't the first time or the last that I fell off a bicycle. I had fallen off when quite small while playing with my brother. He had put me on the carrier and ridden his bicycle across Seven Acres. Nearing a shallow gully that ran across one side of the field he shouted to me, "Hold tight, it is a bit rough and bumpy here," and not receiving an answer found that I had parted company with his bicycle some minutes before. Anyway, once having managed a short trip on my own it soon became easy to balance, and I was a cyclist.

There really was not much danger on the roads as the volume of traffic was quite small compared with the present, and Bert and I were soon allowed to ride round the village and its side roads on Saturdays and during holidays. You will notice not Sunday. Sunday was still a day when you dressed in your best clothes and were allowed to go to Sunday School and for walks, but not much else. Cricket, football and cycling were certainly out. Soon Bert and I began to ride further afield, and he having relatives in the area, we began to visit them. At Punnets Town he had an uncle who was a blacksmith, and we used to go there. I can't remember his aunt's name but she was always good for orange juice and biscuits. Further on at Brightling lived another uncle, who, like Bert's father, was a chauffeur. He worked for some people called Trew at Brightling Park and we sometimes called there to see his Auntie Aggie (I suppose her name was Agnes). Strangely enough I always associate her with singing, as we went to a party once to which several of Bert's relatives came, and in my mind, I can still see and hear her singing, "When the mighty organ played, O Promise Me". From there it was not too far to Dallington, where Bert's grandparents lived. I cannot remember too much about his grandfather, as he seems to have created little impression on me but his grannie was a very nice old lady who always made us very welcome and we were always provided with some of her cake and a drink. On the return journeys we went through Brightling and down a very steep road, Dukes Hill, into the Dudwell Valley. We always tried to go down this hill as fast as possible and without using the brakes. It was probably wildly dangerous but neither of us ever came off and we found it quite exhilarating.

When I was about thirteen, I feel sure it was in the summer of 1937, there occurred an event which has been firmly fixed in my mind ever since. The county eleven were playing Kent at Hastings and another friend, John Fields, was keen to go by bicycle. I got permission to go, and on a brilliant summer's day we set off to Hastings some fifteen miles away. We arrived safely, although cycling in the town was something quite new to us. I remember we parked our bicycles in an underground car park just off the front at a penny for the day. John and I then made our way to the town's cricket ground in Queen's Road where a county week - when two county matches were played - was arranged each year. We paid at the turnstile, entered the ground and settled ourselves down on the front row of seats eager for the fielding team and two opening batsmen to emerge from the pavilion on this, our first day of county cricket. We watched Kent bat until about 1.15 p.m. when John suddenly said to me, "That's Jim Parks sitting in that car," indicating a car parked behind us and to our left. I had a look, and sure enough he was right. This was Jim Parks senior, father of Jim who played for Sussex and England after the war, and grandfather of Bobby Parks, now wicket-keeper for Hampshire. Now I had bought an autograph album for sixpence at Woolworth's some while before and had taken it to the match with me. With encouragement from John, I went across to the car where Jim Parks, who was not playing, was sitting watching the cricket and asked him for his signature, to which he replied without the least enthusiasm, "Not just now, it's almost lunch-time." This seemed a strange answer, as I couldn't understand why he wouldn't sign my book just because it was nearly lunch-time, so I said, "Won't you do it then?" To this question I received a blunt, "No." I never quite forgave him for that. Anyway I returned to my seat and watched the last few minutes of play before lunch. When the umpires removed the bails and the players started to leave the field, I grabbed my autograph book and dashed off towards the pavilion with the intention of asking players for their autographs as they left the field. Unfortunately, in my hurry I ran straight into some old fellow and upended a trug basket of vegetables he was carrying and sent most of them flying.

I've never quite worked out why he brought a basket of vegetables to a county cricket match. By the time I had apologised, been lectured and had helped pick up the produce there was only one player left on the field, a man who had been fielding on the boundary on the opposite side of the ground. I didn't know him but asked for his autograph and he obliged by writing, "R.G. Stainton" on an otherwise blank page. What a disappointment as I'd never heard of him before. It turned out he had been an undergraduate at Oxford University and played for Sussex from time to time. I never forgot him though, as my enthusiasm for autographs waned after that, and his was the only one I ever got from a county cricketer. He was certainly more aware of the enthusiasm of youngsters than Jim Parks, as I got a smile as well as the signature. I can't remember too many details of the day's play but I know I did see Maurice Tate, who was bowling at one end, with Jack Nye at the other. Did ever a pair of opening bowlers have bigger feet than these? I also clearly recall the bowling of Tich Freeman, the tiny Kent leg spinner.

Another activity among boys of my age, and probably among some older and some younger, was the collecting of cigarette cards. Our favourite sets were those of sportsmen. Players issued sets of cricketers in 1934 and 1938, two years in which Australian teams visited this country. I still have these two sets, both of which show James Langridge and Jim Parks of Sussex. In 1938 Jim Parks was described as having a sunny disposition. His disposition didn't seem very sunny the day I spoke to him at Hastings the previous year. If I am correct in thinking this was in 1937, it was the summer when he achieved a record by making over three thousand runs and taking over one hundred wickets, and he scored two thousand odd runs.

Most of the boys who collected cards, had various people whom they used to call upon from time to time with the words, "Any fag cards, please?" There used to be a bit of poaching from time to time as well. One man, a retired policeman, used to keep the cards for me, and how disappointing it used to be when he fished a number out of his waistcoat pocket to find that probably the very ones I still wanted to complete a set, had either creased corners or nicotine stains. Still, there were others who saved their cards for me, which was just as well as I didn't get any from home as father had given up smoking in about 1930, and in any case there had never been any cards, as when he did smoke, it was a pipe.

For some reason, probably the shape of the packets, cards were never, to my knowledge, issued by the tobacco companies with either pipe or cigarette tobacco, but only in the packets of cigarettes. With what we could beg here and there and the swapping of duplicate cards, we usually managed to complete a set. Other interesting sets I collected during the nineteen-thirties were heads of wild animals, butterflies, kings and queens, aviary and cage birds, Derby and Grand National winners, sea fishes, national flags and arms, boy scout and girl guide patrol signs and emblems, and motor cars, all from Players; and wonders of the sea, and railway engines from Wills. It would seem from this list that most of my suppliers smoked Players cigarettes. There was quite a lot of information printed on the back of each card and really we did learn quite a lot from them. Several tobacco companies issued sets of film stars, but we never found these as good as many of the others, for the simple reason that most of us went to the pictures once in a blue moon and didn't really interest ourselves very much in the stars. With sportsmen it was different because we read the sports' pages of the daily papers and we were familiar with the names of famous cricketers, footballers, tennis players, golfers and jockeys. In fact we probably found it easier to recognise a picture of Wally Hammond (England and Gloucestershire cricketer) or Cliff Bastin (England and

Arsenal footballer) than that of the prime minister. Boxers were also sportsmen we knew about although I cannot remember a set of cigarette cards about them. We used to read about boxers, and I know I got up in the middle of the night to listen to a broadcast of the heavyweight championship fight from New York, when Tommy Farr the Welshman only just failed in his attempt to beat Joe Louis. When was that? Again, in 1937 probably.

The Easter holiday from school which naturally fell in the March/April period was, to us, the time to go birds' nesting. Perhaps people are more enlightened nowadays, and most birds' eggs are protected, but when I was a boy there was scarcely a youngster in the village who did not collect birds' eggs. Rightly or wrongly, we learned an awful lot about the different types of birds, where they nested, what their nests were made of, and what they looked like. Three or four of us would go off together armed with small boxes or tins lined with cotton-wool, to search in trees, hedges, banks, ponds and open fields for nests. The tins were for carrying any eggs that we managed to find and which we wanted for a collection.

A warm spring often encouraged the birds to nest early before the leaves appeared on hedgerows and so made the task of locating nests that much easier. At Beechwood the dense area of laurel bushes provided just the right habitat for blackbirds and thrushes. Their eggs were usually left alone after we had put one of each into the collection, as further additions were no longer required. It was still a pleasure to find a nest of hay with a mud lining where rested the bright blue-black spotted eggs of the thrush or the hay-lined nest of the blackbird with greenish eggs blotched with a reddish brown. We usually used to meet by The Stag Hotel and from there follow a public footpath which led across Long Meadow at Beechwood and then across Keith Rowland's farmland to a lane near Southcourt. This lane ran beside hedges for most of its length, which we searched as we went along. Can one ever forget the work of art of a chaffinch's nest, with its moss exterior into which was woven horse hair and feather lining, or the larger nest, also of moss with a hole at the side, of a long-tailed tit? Not far from this path at one place was a pond where each year one could find moorhens' nests. Of course in a country district, many birds were common and their nests easily found, but some were more difficult to find and not easily reached. Others were somewhat dangerous to tamper with. Owls nested in various barns and the pellets which they regurgitated, containing the bones and skin of animals such as mice and voles which they had caught and eaten, were easily found on the ground. To go into barns when owls were nesting and disturb them was a foolish thing to do. Once I heard of a photographer who was taking flashlight pictures of owls when one which he had frightened left the nest and made for the door in panic. As it flew past him a talon caught his eye and he consequently lost the sight of that particular eye.

We had an old ash tree on the estate at Beechwood into which woodpeckers had drilled a hole and made a nest. Now a woodpecker's hole is often drilled horizontally, then vertically, which makes it very difficult to reach the nest as the hole is not big enough to take your arm. Harry Loader, who used to work in the gardens with my father, was always pleasant and ready to help us with anything we were doing. I remember he got a ladder and spent a considerable time with a pliable stick to which was fastened an old spoon attempting to get a woodpecker's egg from the nest. At a later date when the woodpeckers seemed to have gone elsewhere, a pair of jackdaws nested there, and Harry repeated the operation for our benefit.

I cannot recall any of the people who owned the larger houses with quite a lot of land employing a gamekeeper in our village, but pheasants and partridges bred naturally in the area, and we, from time to time, came across the eggs of these birds in their nests on the ground, which are not much more than depressions in the grass. There were also plenty of peewits' nests to be found. The eggs from these were often taken and eaten by the less well off.

Birds' nesting had its funny side. As I have said, nearly all the boys did it although it was discouraged by the police, but whether it was against the law in those times I do not really know. Anyway, three or four boys were out birds' nesting one spring day. One was wearing a flat cap as the part which over-topped the peak was a good place to carry eggs in without breaking them. On their way home on that particular occasion they met the village policeman who, of course, knew them all. "Good morning, boys," he said, and in those more polite days when we had considerable respect for all adults let alone the police, received the reply, "Good morning, sir." "All behaving yourselves?" he went on and the boys chorused, "Yes, sir." "Now you haven't been birds' nesting?" questioned the policeman, probably realising that is just what they had been doing, and received a "No, sir," this time. "Good boys, well done," went on the local bobby, patting the head of the boy with the peaked cap whose face turned a bright crimson as the whites and yolks of several eggs trickled from the cap and on to his forehead.

In order to preserve the eggs in a collection we had to get rid of the contents, and this was usually done by making a hole at each end of an egg, using either a pin or a thorn, then blowing through the two holes which gradually spilled the yolk and white on to the ground. I don't know how much damage we did to bird life by collecting the eggs, but none of the species we knew ever seemed to be in any danger. Looking back, I doubt if we did as much harm as the present method of farming does to bird life through the constant use of chemicals of various kinds.

Barnfield had quite a good cricket team which played on the field which was part of the Beechwood estate and which was available without charge, this being one of the Misses Barrington's contributions to the village social life. It was a pleasant field with the village street running behind a hawthorn hedge to the north. There was also another hawthorn hedge forming the eastern boundary. To the west was the chauffeur's lodge, the drive, and beyond that a plantation of beech and sweet chestnut trees. The ground dropped away to the south to the hedge which separated the cricket field from Drive Field, which was inter-planted in places with some very good oak trees. Members of the cricket team put in a lot of work to keep the ground in good condition, and it was nothing to see several of the men on two or three evenings of the week working on the ground. Nets were erected on one side of the ground, and often a practice session was arranged together with ground maintenance. As boys we were usually welcome on the ground. We took part in fielding practice and also acted as fielders to balls driven through the front of the nets when men were practising batting. Occasionally we were allowed to have a turn with the bat, as generally I think the men took the view that it was a good idea to keep the schoolboys interested, as these would be the players of the future.

We often helped to pull the big roller which was normally used on the wicket the evening before a match was to be played. Sometimes it was decided more weight was required, and as many as half a dozen lads would sit on the wooden framework of the roller while the men pulled it to and fro over the length of the wicket. We often assisted marking out the pitch by carrying out whitening and brushes, and the chain which was used to determine the length of the pitch between the two sets of stumps.

Cricket matches were usually played on Saturday

afternoons once a fortnight with Barnfield team playing away from home when there was no fixture on our ground. Sometimes there were second eleven matches played, or if the first team was not going too far we cycled to a nearby village to watch the game. Evening matches were played sometimes during the longest days of the summer. At Whitsun, and on August Bank Holiday Monday, which was then the first Monday of the month, an all-day fixture was arranged. This meant that we could be at the cricket from eleven in the morning until approximately seven in the evening. Many enjoyable hours did we spend on pleasant summer days, as several of us took a real interest in the matches, and of course we always hoped that Barnfield would win. They often did but sometimes we had to go home disappointed. The village team did have several very useful cricketers when I was a boy and two or three had a trial for the county side.

One man was probably very unfortunate, as he had a trial for the county at the same time as George Cox, and I gather that there wasn't much to choose between them, but as Cox's father had played for the county, young George was given the opportunity. George Cox scored fifty centuries for Sussex during his career, and it would have been interesting to know what the Barnfield man would have done had he had the chance.

The Sussex county team had always been noted for family connections. Apart from the Cox family, Maurice Tate and his father played for Sussex, and also the Gilligan brothers, the Langridge brothers, followed by James' son, the Parks brothers, followed by Jim's son, and the Oakes brothers. Today there are two brothers named Wells playing for the county, and also the Buss brothers played together after the war. Two Cornfords played at one time but they were not related, Cornford being a fairly common name in Sussex.

47

At Barnfield the cricket club had a rather nice pavilion for a village side. It was situated by the eastern boundary of the field, where pads, gloves, stumps, bails etc., were stored as well as the scoreboard. This latter was moved outside on match days. It had three rows of screws on which were hung steel plates with numbers painted on them. The top row showed the score, the second the number of wickets that had fallen, and the bottom row the number of runs made by the last man out. The Pavilion had wooden shutters which pushed outwards and upwards and which were secured by metal arms dropped into sockets. Just inside was the scorers' table. During the matches the home scorer and that of the visiting team sat side by side keeping their books. Each time the score mounted by ten we had a call from the scorer of ten up, twenty up or whatever it happened to be, followed by a mad scramble amongst the boys to put up the plates for the new score. One fellow who used to play when I was a lad, a friend of my father, was a left arm fast bowler, who also had a trial for the county. He was also a big hitter and there was great excitement among the boys when he went in to bat. If he had a successful afternoon it was great to see three or four sixes go crashing into the oaks on the southern side, and I have seen him hit balls out of the ground on the opposite side which crossed the road and fell onto the golf course on the far side.

Between the actual playing area and the road was a rougher stretch of grass. This was cut several times in the summer by a farm mowing machine pulled by a horse which one of the team used to walk about three miles from an outlying farm. By the time they got back to the farm late in the evening no doubt both man and horse were very tired. By the road gate on match days a van owned by Cocoza, an ice-cream seller, used to pull off onto this piece of grass. I assume from his name that he was Italian. He was always much more interested in his customers than the cricket. No matter, to us it was always a treat to be given a penny to take to the cricket in order to buy an ice-cream when Cocoza arrived. A penny then would buy a cornet with a fair dollop of ice-cream on the top. If you wanted an ice-cream between two wafers, that would cost twopence, but much as we wanted we didn't get because we never had twopence all at once.

Humour used to be part of the cricket scene, too. Near where the ice-cream van parked was a flag pole, and on match days a flag belonging to the club was run up to the top of the mast and flew proudly while the cricket was in progress. One Saturday, on arriving for a match we found not a flag at the top of the mast, but somebody's bicycle. The practical jokers of the village had been to work.

Some of the old characters of the village were regular attendees at the matches. One such, an old fellow in his late eighties, used to tell us boys that he had kept wicket for the team years before. This was apparently before the days of gloves and pads, or at least before the players of that time or the club could afford them, and he used to display his old, gnarled hands, explaining that this bump or that swollen knuckle were caused by cricket balls that he had stopped long ago. He had quite an amusing patter, at least we thought so, especially when visiting teams were a bit late in arriving. I can hear him now saying, "They won't come now, sure to. They would ha' been here afore now, if they 'adn't bin comin." He thought what he called modern cricketers were a bit sissy wearing gloves and pads, or as he called them, spats. Heaven only knows what he would have thought of protective helmets. Another of his sayings which I never quite understood but which sounded very very comical was, "If they 'adn't got spats, they'd wear 'em."

Another summer event to which we looked forward was the hay-making season. I don't know why but hay-making always seemed to be later in Sussex than in any other part of the country in which I have lived. It was usually late June or early July before it got underway. It was always exciting to find one sunny, summer morning that as I crossed Long Meadow on the way to school, the contractors were in the field with horse and mower, and to know that when I went home to dinner, much of the grass would have been cut, and it would all be down by the end of the day. The local farmer who rented these fields on the Beechwood estate didn't have a mower of his own, and so used contractors to cut the fields. Not more than one man worked for him, but he did have a horse and a hay cart, known to us as a Sussex wagon. I suppose the wagon was his own, although he could have borrowed it, but he certainly owned the horse. To provide labour for the hay-making he used to use casual workers such as my father, Bert's father, Harry Loader and other men from the village. The work was done in the evenings when they had finished a day's work following their normal occupations.

After the grass had been lying in the sun for a day it was turned with hayrakes, large wooden frames with wooden pegs forming the teeth, and left for another day. It was then raked up, using a rake pulled by the horse, then placed by the men in piles two to three feet high, called haycocks, to finish drying. Once it was in these haycocks it didn't get so wet as it would have done lying loose in the fields if the weather broke. Not that I can remember much rain in the haymaking season. Why do we always remember the summers of our childhood as being hot and sunny?

Boys and girls were to be found in the hay fields in the evenings. We were always full of good intentions and meant to help, but it usually ended with us rolling in the hay and screams of laughter. Happy memories, well except when a thistle penetrated the seat of one's trousers.

In the stackyard at the top of Long Meadow the ground would have been prepared for the stack by placing small branches of silver birch or hazel in a rectangle on the ground so that the hay would not come into direct contact with the soil. Probably they used silver birch as there were two or three birch trees growing nearby. The real excitement for us came when they started carting the hay. The Sussex wagon was a flat cart with fairly shallow sides but these were made much deeper by the addition of extra pieces, much like section of fencing, which were slotted into the sides so enabling a much greater load to be carried. One man stayed on the wagon to pack the hay which was lifted up to him by other men using hay prongs or pitch forks, long handled forks with two curved tines. When the wagon was filled, we pushed and jostled each other to see who would be chosen to help lead Boxer, the brown shire horse, as he pulled the load to the yard where the stack was gradually built. Once the stack reached any height, a man worked on the top to evenly distribute the hay and keep the sides vertical. If the stack was not perpendicular it was likely to topple over during the winter gales, so it was important to get it right. When the stack got above head height, long ladders were used by the men to carry prongfuls to the stacker on the top. This was much harder work than it looked, as a good prongful of hay weighed a considerable amount. Children were not allowed on the stack, as its height plus the sharp tines of the pitch forks meant that it could be quite dangerous. It was always great fun to ride back in the empty wagon to where the next lot of hay was to be loaded.

Probably the greatest thrill of these evenings was late as dusk began to fall, and "Last load home," was called. We were usually given the chance to climb up onto the hay on the wagon for the ride to the stackyard. Then for us it was home to bed. For Boxer it was a tired walk to his stable for his evening meal and night's rest. For the men, usually a visit to the public bar of The Stag Hotel for a pint of Tamplin's beer and a rest at the end of a long, hard day.

Seven Acres was also cut for hay, so the haying lasted for a week or ten days. Depending on the season, one or two stacks were built, and at a later date these would be thatched with straw, a job for an expert, to keep them watertight during the autumn and winter rains. Yes, hay-making was great fun half a century ago, at least for the children. Now the horses and wagons, and more sadly, the men I knew then have all gone for ever. It will never be the same. Can children enjoy what we enjoyed on those long, hot summer days? Surely not with tractor and cutter, baling machine, two men at most and not a buttercup in sight.

We had hop picking holidays in that part of Sussex, as there and over the border in Kent were hop growing areas. This meant that we didn't finish the summer term, which seemed endless when Easter was early, until nearly the end of August, whereas schools in non hop growing districts finished, as now, about the third week in July. This also meant that we didn't start the autumn term until a week or so into October. There were three farmers in the village who had hop gardens. One, Mr Williams, had quite a small area of hops at his farm near Keith Rowland's home, and another, Mr Johnson had a larger garden, both in the Dudwell Valley, but some little way apart. By far the largest acreage of hops was grown by another farmer called Hulme, right out on the extreme north-west boundary of the parish.

As the hops neared ripening stage, and after their size had been taken into consideration, a price for the picking was settled - so many bushels for a shilling (five pence). If the hops were of good size the price was probably seven bushels for a shilling, or if they were smaller it may have worked out at five or six bushels for a shilling. Lists were opened for villagers to book a bin or half a bin during the picking period. Farmers generally paid as little as possible, which meant the lowest rate at which they could obtain labour to pick the crop. There were times when the amount offered was so small that the pickers, much as they needed the money, jibbed at the price offered, and eventually the farmer was forced to offer a little more to save the crop.

The picking usually started early in September, and people decided which farm they wanted to go to according to how long they wanted to work and how much money they planned to earn. If a family wanted to earn just a small addition to their normal income, a woman and perhaps two children would go to Williams' farm where the picking only lasted from ten to fourteen days. If they wished to earn more, Johnson's picking usually went on for three or four weeks, and Hulmes often five or six weeks. In some years children who were working at Hulme's were still picking when the rest of us returned to school.

The bins were about five feet long and two feet wide, and were really a large canvas bag attached to a folding wooden frame. Large families usually booked a whole bin, whereas smaller families would share a bin with another person. These half bins had another piece of canvas through the centre to divide the bin in half. The bins were placed in rows in among the hops ready for the start of the harvest. As hops grow up wires supported by poles, the bines, or long climbing stems, had to be cut or pulled down for picking. On some farms a man would cut down the bines as the pickers wanted them, and on others the workers would pull their own. Children and their mothers, or in some cases, older retired people stood or sat on canvas stools around the bins and snatched the hops from the bines as cleanly as possible, as leaves among the hops were frowned upon by the farmers. Work went on from morning, perhaps about eight o'clock to about five in the afternoon with a break for lunch, which people used to take with them. I helped other people from time to time but regarded myself as fortunate that I did not have to go each day through the harvest period. Mother never wanted to go, and the financial situation at home was such that she didn't have to, and bins were not usually booked out to children on their own.

Even on nice sunny days it was a mucky job and hands became very stained. Children who had to pick came from the hop fields at the end of the day tired, with stained hands and smelling of hops. The smell, although not unpleasant, used to cling to persons and clothing and was not easily got rid of. I'm sure the pickers must have been relieved on any day to hear the cry of, "No more bins to be pulled today," but this must have been doubly so on rainy days. If it wasn't absolutely pouring down, picking went on in the rain, and wet hops made one's skin itch, so it was a case of pick and scratch as well as the discomfort of being wet.

Wet weather was a miserable time in the hop fields. In Kent, at places like Paddock Wood, hundreds of people came from London to pick the hops. They lived in wooden huts provided for them during the season. At Barnfield we saw no one from London, as our hop gardens were much smaller than the Kent ones, and there was enough local labour to do the work. People working at Williams' or Johnson's had to walk to the farms, but because of the distance, Hulme's put on a lorry which picked folks up at different points in the village every morning and brought them back in the evening. During the day, men from the farms used to come round to empty the bins. This was done by packing the hops into a bushel measure and then transferring them to a huge sack called a hop pocket, or poke. After a bin had been emptied, the number of bushels was recorded against the name of the picker, and payment was eventually made when the picking had been completed.

In many homes the money was used to provide new clothes for the coming winter.

Of course, apart from having to work, children who went hop picking missed the fun of playing games, walking or cycling which those of us not picking were fortunate enough to enjoy. An odd day's picking was one thing, but I never fancied doing it for three or four weeks.

Each farm had its own oast houses which were really kilns for drying hops. The pokes, when they were filled, were taken to the oast houses at the farm, where they were manhandled up to the hop floor of the oast and spread out to start the drying process. Later they were shovelled into the drying chamber where they were "cooked" for several hours in the hot air from the furnace. At this time, sulphur was burned, and the fumes went up the chimney with the hot air into the drying chamber, the purpose being to give the hops the colour and smell the brewers preferred. When the hops were dried they were packed as tightly as possible into pokes again, the tops of which were sewn up with twine. The hops were then ready for despatch to the breweries.

In the winter time on some Saturday afternoons we used to take ourselves off to the football field which was in a lane which ran northwards just about half way along the High Street. The field was just beyond the Kings Head, and on the opposite side of the lane. Here Barnfield played their home matches. All the players were familiar faces to us as they were all local men except for a couple of brothers who were schoolmasters at the school attached to St Mary's Roman Catholic Church. They had played in chocolate and green shirts years before my time, but when I was young they played in royal blue shirts and white shorts. Loud cries of "Come on the blues," echoed across the field on match days. The admission fee was fourpence (about 2p) for adults and twopence for children, so as we went once a fortnight, this worked out at one penny a week, the same as we had in summer time to buy our ice-creams.

There was also, I recall, a small group of women who used to go to these matches who used to encourage rough or foul play by cries of "Go on Harry, kick him," or "Come on Fred, put him on the floor." I even remember cries suggesting the referee was short-sighted and ignorant of the rules. On looking back, I believe that some of the players heeded these words of advice from the ladies and gave away free kicks, which did the team no good at all. Sometimes a player was sent off for one or other of these misdeeds, then of course it was the referee who was in the wrong. In one corner of the field was a pond, and I have heard threats to deposit the referee in the same at the end of a match. Barnfield Football Club were on one occasion fined by the league authorities when someone decided it would be a good idea to take the referee's bicycle to pieces and throw them into the pond. This caused quite a rumpus at the time, and both team and spectators were accused of poor sportsmanship. Strangely enough this sort of behaviour seemed to have very little effect on the attitude of the boys who watched but it did seem in very complete contrast to the gentlemanly way in which the cricket matches were played. Of course most of the footballers played to the rules and caused no trouble.

In the late thirties, the football strip being the worse for wear, the team reverted to the old colours of chocolate and green, but cries of "Come on the chocolate and greens" didn't seem to provide the same encouragement as the old chorus of "Come on the blues."

Some of us used to pass the grocer's shop opposite the Stag Hotel on our way to and from school, and it became a bit of a ritual on Wednesdays, I think, to look in one of the shop's windows where they displayed the team list for the following Saturday. It was here I first became familiar with A.N. Other and thought at first someone fresh had moved into the village. Like most teams Barnfield won on occasions and lost at other times, but I believe they had quite a reasonably good playing record during the nineteen-thirties when I saw them play.

CHAPTER FOUR

Although we were never over-burdened with money, twopence (1p) a week being about my spending limit, with a weekly penny for sweets, and a further penny for an ice-cream in summer or twopence for football admission each fortnight in winter, I did have other treats from time to time, as mother seemed to be an exceptionally good manager and found money for various things such as the occasional day out, and some years we actually went away on holiday.

The boys in the village were very lucky to have an excellent scout troop which was run by a generous and enthusiastic man who was a doctor and who had been a colonel in the Royal Army Medical Corps. He had, I imagine, retired early, as he did not work for a living during the time I knew him, but he certainly worked. He stood no nonsense from us and could be quite a disciplinarian, but he was kind and spent much time and I'm sure lots of his own money, and showed great interest in the boys who joined his scout troop. He was a first rate fellow of whom I have extremely happy memories. Looking back I realise how lucky I was to come under his guidance.

He was called Colonel Jenkinson. When I first remember him he lived in a house towards the top of Acland Hill. Opposite the drive gates of Beechwood was a road which was called Brook Lane because it led downhill to a small brook and beyond rose Acland Hill. Next to the house was a hut which he used for the scouts. I can only just remember the scouts meeting there, nor do I know when he started scouting in the village, but presumably sometime after the first world war. When I was quite small he bought a piece of ground in School Lane, some two hundred yards or so beyond the school and south of Mr Johnson's farm house, where he had a house built. This still left a field which stretched from just below his house down to the River Dudwell, on the opposite side of which was one of Johnson's hop gardens. In one corner of the field, beside the road, he erected a scout hut and what a scout hut it was, far better than many town troops have today. It was he who designed it. It consisted of a large room about thirty feet by twenty in three corners of which were smaller rooms without doors, about eight feet square, which were patrol corners and used for patrol activities. There was an entrance hall with coat pegs, and underneath racks for shoes. We were required to change our shoes for plimsolls in order not to spoil the surface of the hall floor. This, I suppose, was a wise precaution, as we often wore shoes or boots with studded heels and soles, and metal heel and toe plates. Opposite the entrance hall at the far end of the main hall, Colonel Jenkinson had an office. On the left of the entrance hall was a woodwork shop, very well equipped which the colonel used for carpentry, which seemed to be one of his hobbies. He was quite good at this sort of thing and made all sorts of things for our use. On the north side of the hall was a doorway leading to the rovers' room, which was about twelve feet square. Both the main hall and the rovers' room were equipped with open fireplaces. Fires blazed in them on winter evenings. I guess that the colonel paid for the coal and wood we used. Over the office and stretching right across the hall and two of the patrol corners was a storage area neatly curtained. It was here that camping equipment, tents, tire bars, dixies and billy cans, pegs, mallets and tables were stored as well as items used in scout concerts. There were facilities for a cub pack for boys of seven to eleven, a scout troop for boys aged eleven to sixteen, and a rover crew for youths of sixteen and upwards and men who continued as members, some into their thirties and beyond. At a later date when there were too many scouts for three patrols, the colonel extended the hut on the south side to make a fourth patrol corner. With all this and the entire field which we were able to use, what more could any troop of scouts require?

Neither was the use of the premises restricted to one night. An official scout meeting was held on Monday evenings, and the hut was open to scouts on Wednesday and Thursday evenings from 7 p.m. to 9 p.m. when all sorts of activities were arranged. The cubs met on Friday evenings from 6 p.m. to 7.30 p.m., and this was followed by a rovers' meeting at 8 p.m. In 1931 when I was seven I joined the cub pack, which was run by a man who worked at an office in the village and lived above it in a flat. His name was Len Gower. He too was an enthusiastic and pleasant man, who gave much of his time for our benefit. We played all sorts of games, did various tests laid down in the scout manual, worked for cub badges and did country dancing. The latter was used as a display item at the summer fete which we held most years. In addition, Mr Gower arranged football and cricket matches from time to time against cub packs from neighbouring villages. These usually took place on Saturday mornings, but sometimes we played a cricket match in the evening on one of the longer days in the summer. I expect at that age we were pretty hopeless, but we enjoyed playing the games. If we were away from home, it was quite an exciting event for us to go on the journey as few of the parents of my friends had cars. We used to travel to these matches by car hired from a local garage or in Colonel Jenkinson's car.

My recollections of the scouts are even clearer, probably because we did much more, and also because memories of early days with most of us tend to be rather obscure. When Bert, several of our friends and I first went to scouts, we seemed rather out of it as the other boys seemed very much older, although some of them were not really so. The fact was we had been sixers and seconds in the cubs, and now we were suddenly very small fish in a much larger pool. To start with, we were called tenderfoots, which certainly didn't make us feel very important, but this feeling soon wore off as we got used to things and to the colonel himself who up until that time we hadn't had much to do with. On winter evenings something in the form of test or games was arranged and time was also spent in our patrol corners working for our second class badges. Six different knots we had to learn to tie, and one or two of these were quite complicated. I recall a reef, a sheepshank, a sheetbend, a clove hitch and a bowline, and I believe the sixth was a round turn and two half hitches. A bowline was quite difficult to learn to tie, then of course there was a granny, which meant whatever it was you were trying to tie you had got it wrong.

We also learned the history of the union flag, and how the flags of England, Scotland and Ireland had been superimposed on each other to form the flag we know today. We also learned signalling by semaphore and using flags we had to send messages to each other. I can still remember the positions of the flags for various letters fifty years on. I recall a game we used to play sometimes when two scouts sat blindfolded some six feet or so apart at the end of the hall, each holding a torch. The rest of us in turn had to creep and climb over various obstacles with the intention of getting near enough to touch one of the blindfolded scouts without his hearing you. If he heard you while you were approaching he shone the torch in the direction of the noise. If the beam fell upon you, you were out of the game. Murder was another popular game we used to play on winter evenings. Someone was very quietly detailed off as the murderer, the lights went out, there then

61

followed a scuffle and a scream, then when the lights went back on someone was lying "dead" on the floor. It was then up to the rest of us by questioning to try to discover who was the "murderer".

Simple first aid was another thing we were taught, and as the colonel was a doctor, the teaching was well done. Lots of emphasis was placed on the treatment of accidents which might occur during scout camps. On summer evenings we practised camping skills, learning how to dig a hole in which a fire was lit using no more than two matches. The fire had iron bars laid across it, and we then tried our hands at cooking. We also had the tents out from time to time, bell tents, nigers and double fours. We learned that pitching tents and properly securing the guy ropes was not quite so easy as it first looked.

We were also taught how to use an axe and make gadgets to hold mugs, plates, cutlery and hats. All these things were learned so that we could cope when we did go to camp. We used to sometimes erect scout staves to which were tied ropes so that we could cross the river at the bottom of the scout field by hanging on to the ropes. The river wasn't very deep but the job had to be done properly in order to prevent the apparatus collapsing when weight was put on the ropes. It never happened to me, but from time to time someone managed to fall into the water to the great amusement of the rest.

On some summer evenings we used to go up to Manor Wood which was situated part way up Dukes Hill where we played what was known as a wide game. Two teams were chosen and we were given coloured paper streamers to attach to our shoulder straps with safety pins. Each team, of course, had different colours. One team went to one side of the wood and one to the other out of sight of each other. The colonel used to start the game by firing his double-barrelled shot gun into the air. We used to then creep about in the wood, using trees and undergrowth as cover until we spotted someone from the other side. The idea was then to dash out suddenly and grab the paper streamer from someone's shoulder. While you were doing this the other boy was probably doing his best to do the same to you. The colonel's gun would bring the game to an end after an hour or so. After we had assembled at a particular spot the paper streamers grabbed would be counted and the team gaining the most would be declared the winners. One night I remember just as it was getting dusk, the colonel, to end the game, put his gun to his shoulder, pointed it skyward and fired upwards into the trees and was much surprised when an unfortunate cock pheasant which had been roosting above suddenly toppled out of a tree and almost landed at his feet.

Colonel Jenkinson was always doing something for the boys in the scouts. On one occasion there was great excitement when we arrived for a meeting and found him struggling at a spot in the field just below a copse, with what appeared to be a large canvas contraption which looked at first like some great tent. After we had helped to spread it out on the ground, it turned out to be a round canvas swimming pool he had bought for us. Ropes were attached to it at eight different places round its circumference and these were then stretched out and secured to wooden poles driven into the ground. When it was filled with water we had great fun that summer, and in subsequent years, as we were allowed to use it during the school summer holiday if the scoutmaster happened to be around in order to supervise us. It was most useful in enabling boys to learn to swim, as the river was too shallow and the lakes at a private estate on the northern boundary of the parish too dangerous. Before the advent of the pool, the only opportunity most of us had to attempt to swim was at the annual summer camp, as the nearest public swimming baths were fifteen miles away.

The annual summer camp naturally cost money, so two events took place during the year to raise funds: an early spring concert in March, and a summer fete, usually in August. I have mentioned that we used to meet, if we wished, on Wednesday and Thursday evenings for other activities. On these evenings some of the time was spent in making things for sale at the fete. One popular activity was making jigsaw puzzles. Interesting coloured pictures were obtained and stuck on to pieces of three-ply wood. When they were completely dry they were cut out as jigsaw puzzles. Simple ones for younger children were done with hand-held fret saws and the more complicated ones were done on a treadle-operated machine which had been obtained for our use. Boxes were found for the puzzles and a title and the number of pieces were written on the lid.

The thing that interested me most was cane work. Somebody came to the scout hut to teach us how to do this and we made baskets and three-ply trays edged with a cane border. These and the jigsaws and various other items were sold at the fete later in the year.

For those not doing things of this sort on Wednesdays and Thursdays there were other activities. We had a trapeze and a pair of gymnastic rings and also a quarter size billiard table and a set of skittles. In addition there were sets of chess, draughts and cards for our use. We had boxing gloves too, and for a while a Captain Shaw came from the village of Northiam to teach us boxing. He had been a light-weight army boxing champion, and I can see him now standing with his arms above his head inviting us lads to hit him as hard as we could in the solar plexus, then saying, "Keep them up, laddie," when we strayed off target.

The concert was an event which took much preparation as the colonel was a great one for having everything about right. Rehearsals used to start before Christmas for the concert in March. It was surprising what talent was available among the rovers, scouts and cubs. We had a rover with a good tenor voice who was very popular singing ballads such as "Bird Songs at Eventide", "Smiling Through", "Passing By", and "I know a lovely garden". His sister used to provide the piano accompaniment. We had another who recited quite well, and yet another who played a saw with a violin bow. In addition we had someone who played the piano accordion and there were at least two more people in the village, not connected with the scouts, who could be called upon to sing in an emergency. We performed various plays. The cubs' plays were often written by Len Gower, and he wrote at least one of the rovers' plays. I recall a retired army captain, who was a keen rover and assistant scout master, writing another. Several of the plays performed by the scouts over the years were written by Ronald Gow. The rovers used to sing an opening chorus and the groups sang the final chorus. On one or two occasions our scoutmaster did a turn by himself. He went down the steps from the stage among the audience carrying a match box in which, he announced, he had a performing flea named Oscar. Oscar was supposed to be able to make prodigious jumps and perform somersaults. He would start his patter by asking whether the people would like to see Oscar jump, and on receiving an affirmative from someone he would open the matchbox a little way, peer inside and say, "Come on Oscar, now do a big jump for the ladies and gentlemen. Now, come along. Ah, that's a good boy. What a magnificent jump." Turning to the audience he would say, "Did you see him?" On receiving the answer, "No," he would say, "Oh well, I'll ask Oscar to do it again. Now watch carefully. Come on now Oscar, another big jump for all the people in our audience. Now come along, be a good boy. Ah, there he goes. Oh dear, he's missed the box. Where are you Oscar?" The colonel would then walk up and down saying in a very concerned tone,

"Oh dear, oh dear, where are you Oscar? Oh, I've lost him. What on earth has happened to him? My poor Oscar." Then all of a sudden he would make a quick movement and grab something from the shoulder of someone sitting near the front where the upper class people of the village were assembled, and with a triumphant cry of, "Oh there you are Oscar," he would appear to slip it back into the match box. He would then look closely into the box again saying, "Are you all right, Oscar?" followed by, "Oh no, this isn't my Oscar." The suggestion that he had picked up a strange flea from one of the elite of the village was not lost on the remainder of the audience.

The concert used to take place on two evenings, Friday and Saturday in about the third week of March following a dress rehearsal on the previous Wednesday, and was held in the village institute which had quite a good stage and a number of dressing rooms as well as a useful-sized room behind the stage known as the parish room. Colonel Jenkinson, was handy with carpentry tools and paint brushes, so most of the scenery we used he made in his workshop at the scout hut. A building firm who owned a lorry was pressed into service to transport large items from the scout hut to the institute. As scouts, we were responsible for selling the tickets which were priced at half a crown (12½p), one shilling and sixpence (7½p) and one shilling and threepence (approximately 6½p). We used to call at houses and do our best to persuade people to buy tickets. So as not to worry folk unnecessarily each scout was allocated a particular area of the village in which to sell tickets. I can't remember too many of the hierarchy of the village actually going to the concerts; perhaps it was beneath their dignity to do so in those times, but usually they bought the half-crown tickets which was probably their way of donating to scout funds. When I think back, if they didn't attend they must have given the tickets away because invariably we had a full house with no vacant seats.

The fete in summer time was held in the scout field. Many of the things made during the winter evenings were sold in the scout hut. In the field we had displays of camping by the scouts, and country dancing by the cubs. There were various side shows, some much the same as those associated with country fetes today, such as coconut shies, hoopla, lucky straws, throwing wet sponges at an aunt sally, skittles and bowling for a pig. We also had a bran tub, a sort of lucky dip for children and Cocoza did not need much persuading to attend with his ice-cream van and donate a percentage of his takings to our funds. One year the rovers fixed up an aerial runway down through the trees of a copse on one side of the field to a place at the bottom near where the swimming pool was situated. It was constructed of small felled trees lashed firmly together with rope in the manner of shearlegs and driven firmly into the ground at either end. Between the two a taut rope was stretched and secured after a pulley had been fitted. For the men, a bar with two handles was suspended from the pulley, and the idea was to grab hold of the handles and push off. As it was all constructed on a slope you just hung on while sailing through the air from top to bottom. This method was considered too dangerous for children and ladies, so a kind of bosun's chair was constructed for them and suspended from the pulley. They just sat in the chair, were pushed away and went down through the trees to the bottom, where there was much padding in the form of old mattresses and canvas to ensure a soft landing. A thin line was attached to the chair, so that the chair, after reaching the bottom, could easily be hauled back to the top. A lot of work went into the construction of the aerial runway and to make sure that it was safe. The charge: twopence for adults, and a penny for children.

From the funds raised, a substantial contribution went towards the annual camp. In 1937 we went to a farm near

Ventnor in the Isle of Wight, for which we paid, if my memory serves me right, seven shillings (35p), and those who were working paid a little more. For this we were transported with all our gear in the local corn-merchant's lorry to Brighton station. From Brighton we went by rail to Portsmouth and from there by ferry to Ryde. I believe we travelled from Ryde to near Ventnor by coach. We had three good meals a day and outings to Alum By, Ventnor and Newport. In camp we played various games (all planned in advance), took part in competitions, swam in the sea twice a day, and did our share of collecting milk and water and doing the cooking. We were awarded points for everything we did or took part in and at the end of the camp one patrol was declared the winner. To us it was a marvellous week, as most of us hadn't been so far from home before. It must have seemed a long way, as when asked by some people in Ventnor where we came from, one boy proudly replied, "England." At this camp the younger boys, of which I was one, first saw the tents we had practised erecting, used in earnest. There were two nigers and two double fours. These were allocated one to each of the four patrols, woodpeckers, peewits, owls and pigeons. The bell tent was erected as a store tent. On this, my first real camp, I also discovered that mallets were not only used by scouts for knocking in tent pegs or making a hollow in the ground to fit your hip bone when lying down, but by patrol leaders on scouts to encourage us to be quiet and go to bed in the evenings. Never mind, it was all very enjoyable and a lot of fun.

In the summer of 1938 we camped at a farm near Corfe Castle in Dorset in lovely countryside. I have never been back to Corfe Castle, but nearly fifty years later I can see it in my mind's eye as though it were yesterday. We travelled there by lorry and train in much the same way as the previous year, and the programme in camp was similar. Outings that year took us to Swanage, to Southampton docks to see the Queen Mary, and to Lulworth Tank Firing Range, where we were guests of the army. I don't know how the colonel managed it, but we went there to see tanks firing at practice targets on the range. Perhaps the army thought the scouts might provide them with recruits in the future. If so, they got more recruits than they had anticipated in the following year. We also went down to Lulworth Cove, where we had rowing boats to take us out into the bay. This was the first time I had ever rowed a boat. Colonel Jenkinson took us out, and as usual lost no time in giving us the opportunity of having a try at something new. Once again we had a thoroughly enjoyable camping holiday. The one small disappointment was that with no sea at Corfe Castle we had no chance to swim. Unfortunately this was my last scout camp, as due to the outbreak of war, the following year's camp was cancelled, and during the subsequent war years we had other things to do.

Two other events of the thirties in which Barnfield scouts played a prominent part were King George V's Jubilee in 1935 and the Coronation of King George V1 and Queen Elizabeth in 1937. Barnfield was keen to be included in the chain of beacons recalling the days of the first Queen Elizabeth when these were used to inform people of the coming of the Spanish Armada, which it was planned to build on these two great occasions. The scouts, in 1935, were asked to help. A gentleman, who owned a piece of woodland almost on the eastern boundary of Barnfield, generously allowed the troop access to his property to fell what timber was required. The woodland in question was really a coppice where trees previously cut to ground level had thrown up a cluster of straight shoots which had grown into useful-sized poles. It was decided that only the rovers should fell these growths and that the scouts should carry them to the roadside. As on other occasions, the local corn-merchant's lorry was pressed into service to transport the wood to the cricket field. A rough patch on one side of the cricket field had been chosen as the site for the beacon, as this was the highest point near to the centre of the village, and also a suitable spot with plenty of room for people to gather on the day when it was to be lit. It was built with a broad base by first putting timbers one way and then the other, and gradually it rose until it was some fifteen to eighteen feet high. Packed in the middle was a barrel of tar to ensure that the beacon would burn even if we had rain before the big day. For a few nights before the jubilee, some rovers camped near the beacon to make sure that no one was tempted to set it off prematurely.

A procession was organised with floats representing different organisations, and the scouts, still using the corn-merchant's lorry, fitted it out with a wigwam and totem pole, and a group of cowboys and Red Indians took their places around these. The procession travelled through the village to the football field, where judging of the floats and a fancy dress competition took place. Following this was an afternoon of races for both children and grown ups, and various other events such as climbing a greasy pole, and tip the bucket. Tip the bucket was a great laugh for the spectators. The participants seemed to enjoy making a spectacle of themselves. A stand had been erected, and from the crossbar swung a bucket of water. Underneath this a horizontal piece of board was attached, with a hole in the middle. A man sat in a wheelbarrow with another one to push him. The one in the wheelbarrow had a pole. The idea was to aim the pole at the hole in the board, which in theory would empty the contents of the bucket onto the pusher. If the man with the pole hit another part of the board, the chances were he emptied the water over himself, which was the result as often as not. Nobody bothered too much what was supposed to happen, but all seemed to have a good time taking part and getting wet. Grand fun for the children watching. At the end of the afternoon we children were given a tea in a marquee erected on the football field. In the evening, as dusk fell, we all gathered in the cricket field. There the beacon was lit and soon created a huge blaze, which we hoped could be seen in the next hill village, Brightling, as we could see their fire. A firework display then took place to round off for us, a very happy day.

As the Jubilee celebrations had been so successful the same programme was followed for Coronation Day. The scouts once again had a hand in building the beacon. Their float on this occasion was made to represent a pirate ship, and we made up the crew. False beards, burnt cork and cutlasses were much in evidence. The youngsters of today who have taken to wearing earrings had nothing on us on that occasion. Ours were mainly brass curtain rings secured with elastic bands. They weren't worth very much but they made up for that in size.

Apart from the annual camps, we sometimes had weekend camps in which tests for first class badges were undertaken. These were also for the development of camping skills, as a patrol took part in the Sussex County Camping Competition at Broadstone Warren during several years in the thirties, and had great success there, winning the competition for three years running.

Proficiency badges could be obtained by passing tests in different subjects. There was quite a lot of competition among the scouts as to who could qualify for most badges. Some went on the right arm of your shirt, and others which helped to qualify for the first class badge went on the left. If you were interested in any particular badge it was never too much trouble for Colonel Jenkinson to arrange whatever was necessary to help you to get it. Bert had lost a certain amount of interest in scouts as we grew older, whereas I had got keener, but I had two other friends, Ron Jeeves and Peter Judd, who were particularly interested in scouting. We three decided that we would like to work for a coastwatchman's badge, not realising how difficult it would be not living on the coast. The colonel fixed up a site for us to camp at and arranged for us to spend time at Fairlight Coastguard Station. He took us down to Fairlight one Saturday afternoon and left us for the rest of the weekend. As there were only the three of us he lent us his own tent which he used at the annual camps. On arrival we pitched the tent, sorted out groundsheets and blankets, and made up the beds. At the other end of the tent we collected together the food we had taken with us, and the cooking pots. Outside we dug a hole for the fire, placed firebars across it, and went off to find sticks for the fire. When we came back some of the wood was covered with an old groundsheet to keep it dry in the event of overnight rain. With the rest we made a fire, boiled a billy can of water to make tea, and had a meal, as we planned to spend the evening and part of the night down at the coastguard station. While we were busying ourselves with the fire and the meal we noticed that in the same field as we had been told we could pitch the tent in, were a couple of horses, shires, which belonged to the farmer. Being country boys we didn't pay too much attention to the horses as we felt that one farm horse was much like another. After the meal we washed up and went off to the coastguard station for our instruction. We found this very difficult to take in as there was so much of it to understand in so short a time. It was, however, very interesting, and we stayed until about two o'clock on the Sunday morning.

When we got back to camp we shone a torch and found that the firebars and billy cans had been kicked all over the place. On examining the tent we found a rent in the wall about three feet long, and a loaf of bread was missing, and other food scattered all over the tent. Vandals were practically unknown to us in those days and we soon realised that the horses had been back and had kicked the hole in the tent. We knew that our loaf was safely inside a

72

horse. After examining the mess and the rent in the canvas, we were thankful that no one had been sitting or lying in the tent at that spot when the horse's hoof came through.

After spending more time at the coastguard station on Sunday afternoon we returned to our field to strike camp and pack up the equipment ready for when the colonel came to fetch us. Somewhere about six o'clock in the evening I went down to the farm to return the milk can, as they had supplied us with milk. As I came out of the farm garden gate into the lane, along came the colonel in his car. He slowed up and shouted, "Come on, jump in. I'll take you up to the camp." As I got in he continued, "Had a good weekend? Everything all right?" I said, "Yes, thank you, we've had a good weekend, but unfortunately there were horses in the field we camped in." "Nosey creatures, horses," observed the colonel, and with a huge grin added, "They kicked a hole in the tent I suppose." "Well," I replied, "we're a bit worried about that because as a matter of fact that is just what they did do." He slowed down, looked at me as if it were our fault and bellowed, "What?" I looked at him again and went on, "Yes, I'm afraid the horses did kick a hole in your tent." His moment of bad temper passed as quickly as it came, then he observed, "Oh well, no doubt it can be repaired, but I was rather fond of that tent." As we had found things pretty difficult at the coastguard station we decided not to pursue the idea of getting that badge, and just let things die a natural death.

After war broke out, the scouts took on the job of collecting waste paper. When a fire brigade had been formed in Barnfield some years before they at first had a hand cart on which to push their equipment. When they eventually got a fire engine they gave the hand cart to the scouts. We had used it as a trek cart to carry our camping equipment when we had gone for weekend camps not too far away from home. We now used it to collect the paper and set a night a week aside to go calling for it.

Peter and I and a few others walked miles as we went to outlying farms and houses to gather up the paper they had saved for us. One week we would go in one direction, another week in another direction, and so gradually we got round the parish. We had a shock on one occasion when we called at a fairly large house in the village near the church, where lived two unmarried sisters who were no longer young. I knocked on the door and when one of the ladies opened it I said, "We're scouts and we've called for any waste paper." She replied, "I'm afraid there is rather a lot. You see, my sister and I have talked it over and we have decided we must be patriotic and help the war effort, so they will have to go. Could you come up to the attic and have a look?" We went, we looked, and there were piles and piles of newspapers, in fact a copy of the Daily Mail for each day, except Sundays, throughout the first world war, which was well over thirteen hundred newspapers. We moved them all to the scout hut, and as they seemed to be thicker papers than we had in the second world war, we certainly didn't get them all on the cart at one go. We were thankful we had discovered this little hoard within half a mile of the scout hut and not at one of the outlying farms. Mind, we found them extremely interesting and spent as much time reading them afterwards as we had done collecting them.

CHAPTER FIVE

Most of my friends and I went to Sunday School each week. It was the accepted thing in those days, and all told, we quite enjoyed it. There was a short service for all of us, then we divided up into groups according to age and were told bible stories by various Sunday School teachers, a group of rather nice ladies who usually managed to hold our interest. These and the scripture lessons we had at school at least gave us a basis for decent living in which the needs of other people were emphasised. This way of life was reinforced at home, and I cannot recall any of the boys I knew well in those days getting into any serious trouble, neither then nor afterwards.

At Sunday School we each received a stamp book. Coloured stamps showing scenes from the life of Jesus were given out to us at the rate of one per week. If you were absent because of illness you would be given back numbers, but not if you were absent without good reason. From our point of view it was important to get a particular number of stamps in the book each year, forty-eight out of fifty-two I believe, because two things dear to our hearts depended upon it. First was prize giving, which occurred round about Christmas, and usually took the form of a book. Whoever chose them did quite a good job, as we were pleased, most times, with what we received. I recall "Treasure Island" and "A Life of Christ", written by Charles Dickens for his own children.

The other important event to which we looked forward with a great deal of pleasant anticipation was the Sunday School outing. We went to the same place each year, Hastings, and we were always anxious to get there, because although we did not live all that far from the sea, it wasn't very often that most of us went to it. Children who had made the necessary number of attendances at Sunday School went free. Parents could also go if they paid, which many of them did. I expect the organisers were glad to have extra grown ups to look after some of the children.

Bert's family and mine were friends, and we usually went together. There would be Bert's mother, his sister, and my mother, Bert and I in a little group. Sometimes my father would have a day off work and go as well, but I cannot remember Bert's father ever going. Perhaps that sort of thing didn't appeal to him. We would assemble by the church, as there was a convenient spot for the coaches to turn round, at nine o'clock. After lists had been checked we used to clamber aboard one of the coaches, there were usually two, and away we went. It took about three quarters of an hour to reach Hastings, but we looked forward to the coach ride, as this was pure enjoyment to us as we went so seldom. We used to take a packed lunch with us, but tea was arranged for us at a local restaurant. On arrival we were given instructions as to where and when to meet for tea. It was always the same place, Lewcock's cafe on the sea front. After this we were away to the beach. I say beach, as many Sussex seaside places have a considerable amount of shingle, and one has to wait for the tide to go out before you can reach the sand. This is true of Hastings, and years later while sitting in a barber's shop waiting my turn for a haircut, I was listening to the barber talking to the man whose hair he was cutting. The customer said to the barber, "Are you going away for a holiday this year?" This was in a midland town, and the barber answered, "I was thinking of going down to the south coast, to Hastings." At this, the man in the chair said, "I went to that bloody place for my holiday last year. It might have been popular with visitors since 1066, but you still have half a bloody mile to walk to reach the sand." With patience, which we didn't show too much of, eventually all was revealed and the sands were ours. In our younger days we had buckets and spades. These were carefully put away from year to year, and taken out for day trips of this kind. Sandcastles were the usual thing, and Bert and I would soon be busy filling buckets and constructing walls and towers. This was followed by digging a moat and filling it with bucket after bucket of water. The buckets weren't very big, so this task took us some time. By the time a castle was built there were cries for us to come to lunch. This never appealed to me particularly. There were always hard-boiled eggs, which I wasn't keen on and somehow or other sand always seemed to get mixed up with the sandwiches. This dislike of packed lunches stayed with me when I grew up, and I always then preferred a visit to a cafe rather than taking a sandwich meal. Mother, of course, wouldn't have considered this idea, as she would have regarded cafe meals as far too expensive.

I was not very popular at lunch time on one of these outings, as mother had asked me to put some salt into a screw of grease-proof paper to take with eggs. Of course I had a better idea than that, and decided an envelope would be neater. Unfortunately the salt seemed to unstick the envelope, and when lunch time arrived mother found that salt had got mixed up with the buns. Mother had quite a moan about this, and I got a lecture about doing things the way I was told. I told her that I didn't mind salty buns, which wasn't strictly true, and father, I'm sure, was not in the least worried over such a little thing, but she was not to be placated for some while afterwards. When lunch was over it was then off with our shoes and stockings and into the sea for a paddle, accompanied by a chorus of instructions from careful parents. "Be careful, look what you are doing. Don't go out too far, it's dangerous. Don't dash about, there may be holes you cannot see." Followed by, "Take care there isn't any broken glass." In spite of all these instructions we enjoyed our paddling and nothing seemed to happen to any of us. We would stay there, having fun, until we were called to come and dry our legs and feet, and get our shoes and stockings back on. This was something of a problem, as it always seemed to be a struggle to get into the calf length stockings we then wore, when our feet were not completely dry. Having dried one's feet they got damp again as soon as they came into contact with the sand, and moving up on to the shingle didn't help, as there always seemed a coating of sand there. We sat and struggled only to find that heels of socks were in the wrong place and wouldn't go comfortably into shoes. After a time, however, all was accomplished and we were satisfactorily shod, and ready to go off to find the promised ice-cream. After that we usually went down into the town to look at the shops so that our mothers could buy a few things rather cheaper than they could at home. To Bert and me, Woolworth's was always the main attraction, as we didn't have shops like that in the village, nor did we usually see a display of goods like they had. Woolworth's in those days was a threepenny and sixpenny stores, but you could usually find something of interest for less than that. Anyway, this was a special day and we had money to spend, at least sixpence (2½p), and we felt rich. How long we spent trying to make up our minds is nobody's business, but we had to select carefully, as we knew that a similar opportunity would not present itself for some time to come. After that it was usually time to gather for tea. It wasn't long before we started to see familiar faces all making for the same spot. They used to do us well for tea at Lewcocks. We had sandwiches, followed by an attractive assortment of cakes, which I don't suppose were as good as those mother made, but they were different, and certainly tempted us.

These were followed by something like jelly and ice-cream served in glass dishes. All this was washed down with orange juice. At least the children had orange juice, while the grown ups preferred tea. After leaving the cafe, the coaches would be waiting to take us home. It never seemed to rain, and we would reach home tired and happy with plenty to talk about for days to come.

Mother had come from Yorkshire, and when she and my father married they went to live in Kent where he worked at that time. When they moved to Barnfield she fell in love with Sussex, preferred it to Kent, and never had the slightest desire to return to Yorkshire, although strangely enough, she was never slow to tell people that she was a native of that county. Eastbourne was her favourite spot by the sea. She and father, and of course I nearly always had a day there during the summer months. One could get to Eastbourne by bus. A bus travelling from Barnfield to Brighton passed through Heathfield where one had to change. From there a bus ran through Horam, Hailsham and Polegate, and then on to Eastbourne. On the journey, mother and father used to examine gardens which they passed, and most of the conversation was about flowers and other plants which they noticed.

It was a quieter day than a Sunday School outing because mother and father both worked hard and they just wanted to relax by the sea for a few hours. We used to alight from the bus outside Eastbourne railway station, then we would have a leisurely stroll up to the front, doing a bit of shop gazing, as mother called it, on the way. Occasionally mother would buy a few things, especially if there was something she wanted that was cheaper than in the village. We would then stroll along the promenade, and afterwards settle on a seat, just watching other people and gazing at the sea and whatever was happening. After a lunch which we had taken with us it was a walk to the bandstand where they would sit for a while, listening to the band. Another walk along the front, a visit to a cafe for a cup of tea, then it was time to make our way to the depot where the homeward bus left from. Perhaps this doesn't sound a very exciting sort of day for a youngster, but I used to enjoy it, mainly I suppose because it was a treat to leave the village for the day, have a bus ride, and see something else. I was happy enough in the village but a change of scene for a few hours was always welcome. As I grew older I was able to leave mother and father sitting somewhere while I went off to see what I could see or find which was of interest.

Perhaps children of today would regard it as a tame outing, but maybe they are more demanding. We were, I imagine, rather more easily satisfied. No doubt it is all relative. When you didn't have very much you were very pleased to have just a little more.

Twice during my childhood we spent a week's holiday at Eastbourne. On the first occasion I was only about five, so do not remember too much about it. I do know that we stayed with a Mr and Mrs Grice, and that we provided our own food which Mrs Grice cooked for us. Mother certainly didn't intend to pay Eastbourne prices for vegetables if she could help it, so when we set off, father had a large suitcase with our clothing and other belongings in it, and in addition, a large bag of vegetables. On arrival we went to Mrs Grice's boarding house, somewhere in Seaside, saw our room, deposited our things and then went shopping for groceries of one sort and another, which were then taken back to the boarding house where some were handed over to Mrs Grice. Some like butter, sugar, jam and biscuits were stored in the sideboard of the room where we were to sit and have our meals. During the shopping, my brother Ted, who was also with us, decided he would like some greengage jam. At home we always ate the jam that mother made, and really Ted and I knew little, if anything, about jam bought from shops. I think he was attracted by the colour, a brightish green, which only put mother off. She tried to dissuade him but he still fancied it, and in the end it was purchased. When we did eventually get round to trying it his verdict was, "Tastes like Vaseline." It certainly didn't taste anything like the greengage jam that mother made from the fruit from our own tree.

I do recall during this holiday going off with my brother when mother and father were sitting on the front. I seem to remember having nothing on my feet, but where we actually went or what we did I cannot now recall, but we were away for about one and a half hours. By the time we returned mother had worked herself into some state wondering where on earth we were or what had happened to us. Father, as usual, was quite unmoved. Did he ever get concerned or worried about anything? Not that I remember. He always appeared to me to be quietly spoken, good tempered and a man who never got excited or bothered about anything. On the other hand, one word from him and we did what we were told.

The second time we went to Eastbourne was when I was about eleven, I suppose. This time I was alone with my parents, as my brother by then was at work. We stayed with Mrs Grice again, but I believe it was at another house, as I think she had moved in the intervening years. I know we stayed on the same basis of providing our own food while she did the cooking. this seems odd to me now but I believe it was done regularly by people holidaying during the thirties. I recall rather more about this holiday, as it was during that week that I went to the cinema, or the pictures, as it was then known, for the first time. Actually I went twice and saw Greta Garbo in "Queen Christina" one night, and "The Prisoner of Zenda" another. I believe that talkies had not been long commonplace at that time, as one of the supporting films I saw was silent. This I found most amusing and can still see in my mind one episode. A man and a woman went down to the edge of a lake where a rowing boat was moored. They both clambered in and sat down, the man taking the oars. The woman undid the painter and the man started to row, but it appeared that the woman had caught the bottom of her jumper, which was obviously hand-knitted, on a nail driven into the post to which the boat had been tied. Of course, as the boat was rowed away, the wool of her jumper began to unravel row after row. The further the boat went the less jumper she had left. Stretching across the water from the boat to the shore was a very long piece of wool. This may not sound very funny now but to an eleven year old watching it, it was hilarious.

Mother was fond of going up to Beachy Head and getting what she described as a good sea blow. One afternoon we caught the open-topped double decker bus up to Beachy Head. We walked across the short green turf towards the edge where the cliffs fall away abruptly to the sea and from where one can look down on the lighthouse. Without going too close, we sat down and gazed at the shipping passing to and fro along the Channel while mother got her ration of sea breeze. I had been told by mother to stay with them, as she regarded the area as far too dangerous for me to go off on my own. She was probably right, although there was a wire fence a few feet from the cliff edge. After a while I imagine I got a bit bored just sitting, and was kicking my feet against the turf when I disturbed what appeared to be and was a small piece of chalk, because of course these cliffs along the Sussex and Kent coasts are all chalk. It occurred to me that a piece of chalk would write, so without her noticing it I wrote 1/6 (7½p) on the sole of my mother's shoes. She sat there for sometime with her legs stretched out in front of her. Several people passed by, gazed at her shoes and smiled. One lady who looked in her direction burst into laughter as she went by. This reaction became noticeable, and mother said to father, "What are they laughing at, Syd? Is it something to do with us, as people keep grinning as they pass." He had a look round, and of course eventually spotted the chalk mark. He said, "Well Nance, if I were you, I would get my shoes paid for." After this remark she pulled off a shoe only to find the 1/6 on the bottom. She too saw the funny side of it then.

Another afternoon we went on a mystery tour though the Sussex countryside. It looked at one time as if we were going to stop for tea at Barnfield, but in the end we turned off a few miles short of the village and went on elsewhere, which was really a good thing, as tea at Barnfield wouldn't have been much of a mystery. The only mystery would have been where in Barnfield we were to have tea.

While at Eastbourne that week we visited the redoubt, a fortification which was built for the defence of the town in the Napoleonic wars, and the Wish Tower, which is really a Martello Tower, also built during the period of threat of an invasion from France. Below the Wish Tower was the Eastbourne lifeboat station. There are some quite interesting gardens at Wannock, where apart from the flowers, a number of animals are kept, and we spent an afternoon there. Anchored off Eastbourne during our stay was HMS Malaya, showing the flag in a navy week visit. Small boats, called naval cutters, took visitors out to the battleship, and as father had served in the navy during the first world war it was only natural that we should go on a tour of inspection. Members of the crew welcomed us at the top of the gangway, and others showed us around the ship, which I found most interesting. I was impressed by the size of her, certainly by far the biggest ship I had seen at that time. We ended up by sampling the navy's home made ice-cream. As we left the ship to return to the shore I little dreamed that within the space of a few short years I should be much more familiar with the Royal Navy. Mind, I never saw ice-cream again on a ship until I went aboard a US aircraft carrier in Colombo harbour towards the end of the war. I'm afraid my friends and I thought they were rather soft with their ice-cream machines and soda fountains.

We managed one more holiday before the war, which was to prove more of an adventure for me than anything that had gone before, because as far as I was concerned we were breaking into fresh territory. It must have been 1936 that father and mother decided to go to Birmingham during September to visit mother's sister, and my Aunt Blanch. I had seen her once when I was very small, when she and my two cousins had stayed with us at Beechwood, but it was not for very long. My aunt and elder cousin, Eileen, had apparently drunk some milk at some point on the journey down, and both had been taken ill and ended up in Tunbridge Wells hospital. Marjorie, her younger daughter, had not had any of the milk and was all right, so she stayed with us. Shortly after my aunt was discharged from hospital, they returned to Birmingham so my memories of them in 1936 were rather vague to say the least. My Uncle Jack came down on the back of his brother's motor cycle to see my aunt, but apart from the fact that they had arrived very late, had had considerable difficulty in finding Beechwood, and when they had located it they couldn't find our cottage and had slept the night in the potting shed, I could remember nothing of him. So really, apart from strange territory, it was to be a holiday for me among strangers.

Strangers or not, it turned out to be a good holiday which I thoroughly enjoyed. Of course this meant travelling via London, which in those days provided excitement in itself. We crossed London from Charing Cross to Euston by cab, the first time I had been in a London taxi. The non-stop journey from Euston to New Street, Birmingham took a couple of hours, the longest train journey I had done at that time. We were met on arrival by Auntie Blanch and also Auntie Alice, mother's other sister who also lived in another part of Birmingham. After the greetings were over, we travelled by bus from the station to Kings Heath, where Auntie Blanch and Uncle Jack lived. I didn't see too much of my cousins in day time as this was a September holiday as usual, and Marjorie's summer holiday was over. She was back at school, and Eileen had by this time started work and was out all day.

We did all sorts of things that week which I had never had the opportunity of doing before. We went on a trip on the outer circle bus route which took us all round the outskirts of Birmingham and through places I had never seen before. I particularly remember going through Edgbaston on the way into the city centre on another day. Edgbaston to me meant cricket, and I knew that Warwickshire's county ground was there. Had it not been at Edgbaston in the year of my birth that two Sussex players, Maurice Tate and Arthur Gilligan, while playing for England had bowled out South Africa for a mere thirty runs, eleven of which were extras? Gilligan had taken six wickets for seven runs, and Tate four for twelve in forty-eight minutes. The ball used was so unworn that the manufacturer's name could still be read at the end of the innings.

In the city centre we shopped in Corporation Street, which to my mind was hot and crowded compared with the peace of Barnfield High Street which I was used to. However, I found the Bull Ring more interesting with the barrows of street traders and the cries of their owners encouraging one to buy.

We also visited the art gallery in town, where I

remember bags and umbrellas being collected from us at the entrance. I don't recall much about the actual pictures but remember that umbrellas were banned in the gallery to prevent people waving them about and possibly damaging the canvases.

Another very exciting trip was to Bourneville, which is quite near to Kings Heath, where we visited Cadbury's chocolate factory. I had never seen anything like this before, and rather envied the girls, all in white overalls, surrounded by chocolate. We were told about the cocoa beans coming from overseas. Whereas most cocoa beans came from what was in those times Gold Coast, now Ghana, I seem to recall that most of Cadbury's was imported from South America. We were shown the complete process of roasting and crushing the beans, the extraction of a certain amount of cocoa butter before the chocolate was made, and also how various chocolates were hand-decorated with various utensils resembling forks. What I found really intriguing was the plant where paper bags were placed in cocoa tins, a measured amount of cocoa put in the bags, the tops turned over, coupons placed on top, then the lids of the tins put on, the tins turned over and a label wrapped round each, all by machine.

Probably the most enjoyable event of the holiday, for me anyway, was when I persuaded my father to take me to a league football match. I had never seen a league match, and discovered on reading the sports pages of the daily paper that on the Wednesday while we were there, Birmingham were playing an evening match against West Bromwich Albion. As this was a first division match I was particularly keen to see it, and, as Uncle Jack quite liked the idea, it was decided we should go to St Andrews, Birmingham City's home ground. I opted to support West Bromwich, and had my leg pulled as it seemed my uncle was a Birmingham supporter. I was suitably impressed by the size of the ground and the stands, and had to admit it was all rather more sophisticated than Barnfield's ground. To me it was a cracking game ending in a draw of one goal each. Sandford scored for West Bromwich, but I no longer have any idea who scored the Birmingham goal. A draw, I suppose, was a good result, as among supporters honours were at least even. I didn't see another first class match until I did a course in London during the war, and was then able to see a few games at White Hart Lane. These of course were war time matches and not quite up to the pre-war first division standard because not all the best players were available. I still have happy memories of that first visit to Birmingham, and though I have been back there many times since, I never got the same thrill again as I did on that first occasion.

Now and again during my boyhood we made journeys to Tunbridge Wells, but these were mainly shopping expeditions. A bus ran from Barnfield three or four times a day. We would travel on that when we went. Sometimes, if we went on a Saturday, father would come, but at other times I would go with mother on a weekday during the school holidays. Various things such as tea and sugar could be obtained more cheaply than in the village, and mother would stock up with these. She would also buy bacon, meat and butter, items of clothing and household items such as towels, tablecloths, sheets and pillow cases if these were needed.

The return fare for adults was half a crown (12½p) return, and mother always aimed to cover the fare and save a bit more while she was in Tunbridge Wells. I have perhaps given the impression that mother was tight with money but that isn't strictly true, as most working class families went on in the same way in those times. There was never very much money to spare. We always lived quite well, but mother never paid more than she had to for anything, as apart from providing us with what was necessary she liked, as she used to say, to put a little away for a rainy day. She once told me that the vicar had given her this piece of advice when she and father were married.

Sometimes when we went on Saturday we would stay late and go to a cinema before leaving on the last bus for home. This went soon after nine o'clock from the war memorial and only ran on a Saturday. It was always crowded, and some people would get off in Frant Road, a road leading out of the town into the Sussex countryside which was no more than a mile or so from the departure point. After someone from Barnfield was left behind, they changed the system. Barnfield was as far as the bus went, and after this person was forced to spend the night in Tunbridge Wells, an inspector would turn up at the stop and call for folk going to Barnfield to board the bus first, then people from other villages along the route. This meant that anyone left behind was probably trying to get to Frant Road, and there were other buses that went to that part of the town.

One other memory of outings is when we went to Eastbourne on a Saturday soon after Christmas one year in the mid thirties to attend a pantomime at one of the theatres. It was Jack and the Beanstalk, and proved to be a glorious couple of hours of slapstick comedy. Apart from the story there seemed to be scenes just put in for the laughs. I have never seen as much china broken as they smashed in a plate-throwing scene, and at that time I had never seen as much china all in one place at one time. I had never seen a pantomime before, but afterwards looked forward eagerly to the next, which I'm afraid didn't come until I was an adult, and therefore was not quite the same.

CHAPTER SIX

What else did we do as children in a village where apart from scouting we did not have much laid on for us but had to make our own amusements. Well, several events took place in the year which attracted our interest. One seemed to meet all one's friends at these, which wasn't really surprising, as nearly every boy in the village attended each.

Barnfield had a nine-hole golf course, the land on which it was laid out being owned by two sisters who lived in a fair-sized house almost opposite the cricket field. The golf course itself had an entrance almost opposite the drive gates of Beechwood, and the course went downhill beside and parallel to Brook Lane. On the other side of the brook the ground rose, and here the course was adjacent to Acland Hill. Just inside the gates was a sort of natural hollow where members and visitors used to park their cars. At the top of the bank at the village side of this hollow was the club house, first tee and ninth green. Twice during the year, usually once during the Easter holiday and again during the summer holiday, a tournament of three days' duration was held. These we looked forward to very much as it gave us the opportunity to earn a few shillings caddying for golfers playing in the various events. Bert and I would go early, but it seemed every other boy from the village had the same idea, and it was a case of chasing after each car as it arrived. As soon as it stopped there was a chorus of, "Caddie, sir?" or "Caddie, madam?" Gradually boys got jobs. Sometimes we found ourselves without a job, and this was a great disappointment, as no job of course meant no money. The pay wasn't great. We used to carry the clubs, if we had a job, round the nine holes twice in the day. Once round in the morning and again in the afternoon. The set amount for this work was sixpence (2½p) a round, so we earned a minimum of a shilling (5p) a day. Some golfers were more generous and paid a little extra. One dear old lady always used to say to her caddie at the end of the day, "There you are sonny, sixpence a round and a penny for sweets." I caddied a couple of times for a retired army major who lived as a permanent resident at a guest house in the village. He was of uncertain temper. I never did very much to please him. He would slice a ball into the rough or into the woodland, then moan loud and long if I couldn't find it, and lecture me on the high price of golf balls. I used to think to myself, "Well it's not my fault - you hit it to wherever it now is," but of course I said nothing. Sometimes it was, "Don't stand there boy. You are distracting me," or even when I was out of sight he would suddenly round on me and shout, "Stop fidgeting, boy. Stand still," although I was probably not moving at all. One got used to the clubs players would use for different shots, so at times I would walk across to him and pull from the bag the club I thought he would use. On occasions he would take it from me with, "Not that one, boy," and ram it back in the bag, sort them over and finally extract the same club I had just offered him in order to play his stroke. I could put up with being grumbled at as it was the old story of, "Sticks and stones may break my bones, but hard words never hurt anyone." Strangely enough, at the end of the day his attitude changed completely, and he would say to me as he paid, "Thank you boy for being so helpful," and you would find in your hand not one shilling but one shilling and sixpence. In spite of his sharp tongue I would have been happy to caddie for him more often but he didn't always play, and when I had the offer of a job for each tournament I accepted it.

Bert came dashing down to our cottage one night and said, "We've got to go to see Miss Ingram up at Acland House." I asked, "When?" He replied, "Now, come on." "What's it all about?" I enquired. Bert went on, "She wants to see us both. It's something to do with golf I think. She left a message at my house." Now two sisters lived at Acland House, which was right at the top of Acland Hill on the left. Bert had caddied a time or two for the younger Miss Ingram. She seemed to like Bert and she knew that we were friends. So off we went to Acland House, which was the best part of a mile from our place. When we got there we were asked inside and both the Misses Ingram came into the room. They apparently thought we were polite and willing and we were asked if we had a caddying job for the forthcoming tournament. On being told, "No," they offered us jobs on a more or less permanent basis. There would be no rushing after the people seeking work. Bert would caddie for the Miss Ingram he had been with before and I would do the same for her elder sister. They were pleasant ladies and we got on very well with them. Actually I didn't lose any money because about this time there was a meeting of what I suppose was the golf committee, and it was decided that in future caddies should be paid ninepence (just under 4p) a round. The Miss Ingram I worked for decided after a day or two that the bag appeared to be rather heavy for me, and as she didn't use all the clubs regularly she would reduce the number from eleven to seven, which I must admit, made the bag more comfortable to carry around for five hours or so a day. Golf clubs did weigh quite a lot especially the steel-shafted ones that seemed to be gaining in popularity just then. Added to the weight of the bag and clubs were spare balls, tees, ball cleaners, and probably gloves and a Mackintosh. Neither of the Misses Ingram was a great player and between them they lost balls fairly regularly. In the past we had wandered round the golf links after a tournament searching for balls that had been lost.

These, if we found them, we would sell to the groundsman for a penny each. I expect he sold them back to the players for more than a penny. Anyway after Bert and I started working for the Misses Ingram, we sold the balls we found to them and they gave us twopence for them, sometimes threepence if a ball was in exceptionally good condition. I believe to buy a new ball one had to pay at least sixpence in those days.

Working for these two ladies got better still, as they sometimes went over the county border into Kent to play at Hawkhurst, and we were asked to go with them. The Miss Ingram Bert caddied for drove the car so the two bags of clubs went into the boot, Bert and I went into the back and the two ladies travelled in front. On the first trip to Hawkhurst we were given at lunch time a packet of sandwiches, a piece of cake, a flask of tea and cups while the ladies went off to the club house for their lunch. The sandwiches and cake were very good, but when we came to drink the tea, neither of us had ever tasted anything like it. We thought it was awful. Fortunately Bert had found a sixpenny piece in the grass during the morning so we nipped along to the nearest shop and had a bottle of ginger beer each. When I got home mother asked, "What sort of a day have you had?" As we had been paid two shillings (10p) for the day because of the time travelling, I said, "Oh, jolly good except for the tea at dinner time." "What was wrong with that?" mother enquired. I replied, "It was awful stuff. I've never tasted tea like it before and neither has Bert." Mother suddenly grinned as she said, "I expect it was China tea." I'd never had China tea before or as a matter of fact since. Next time I saw Bert he said, "Mum said it was China tea we had." I said, "Yes, my mum said exactly the same." So our mothers were agreed that it was China tea and we were also agreed that we didn't like it.

Both Bert and I bought golf clubs, only one each, from

the groundsman at Barnfield Golf Club, and we used to spend some evenings hitting golf clubs round the edge of the cricket field. I think we were quite keen on the game at that time, but neither of us ever played after we grew up. Sometime during the late thirties, we were dealt a bit of a blow when the ladies who owned the golf course decided to sell their house and build a new one somewhere near where the club house stood, and close the golf club. A piece of the course was fenced off for their garden and the rest of the ground was let to local farmers for grazing land. After this decision had been made bang went our chance to earn the odd shilling. Rumour had it that there had been some disagreement among the club members, and the owners not liking what they had heard, decided to build this new house, and that would automatically end the days of the golf club. Not that I was ever allowed to spend the money I earned, as after a tournament I was directed to the post office along with my bank book to pay in my three days' pay of three shillings, or later, four shillings and sixpence.

The Methodist Chapel in the High Street had evenings occasionally when they showed lantern slides. Someone would give a talk, and although we were both church members, Bert and I, and many other children were always made welcome by the pastor. Looking back, I felt more at ease with him than I did the vicar at St Mark's. Strangely enough whilst I was overseas in wartime I received a copy of the new testament from the chapel but not a word of any sort from my own church. To get back to the story these evenings were sometimes about life and work in countries far overseas where missionaries had been working and now and again we had lantern slides dealing with natural history. When I say slides I am not referring to 35 mm slides which are so common today. These were made of glass and measured about three inches square, and were shown in a cumbersome projector known then as a magic lantern. Nevertheless, the quality of the pictures was remarkably

93

good and we had some enjoyable evenings watching them. At the end of the talk and show we used to sing a few hymns and the pastor said a few prayers. Before we left we often used to sing, "I'm H.A.P.P.Y., I don't know why I'm happy, I only know I am." Come to think of it we were happy and I doubt if we could have explained why had we been asked.

Towards the end of a summer holiday, about the first week in October, on a grey and miserable day with intermittent rain, Bert and I were near the church when along came a hearse complete with coffin, followed by a couple of other cars. We, I suppose, at that time were eight or nine years old and had never been to a funeral, so as the weather wasn't very nice for playing out we decided to attend. We waited until a stream of mourners, some from the cars and others who had arrived on foot had entered, then we followed and sat down towards the back of the church. We listened to the service and I know they sang "Abide with me" but we couldn't follow the service properly or really join in the hymn because we didn't have either prayer book or hymnal. We were gazed at by several people, but as we were not misbehaving nobody asked us to leave, but no one offered books. I think that the sidesman, although he didn't say anything, took exception to our presence, and so chose to ignore us. When, at the end of the service they carried the coffin from the church, we again followed the mourners round to an open grave in the churchyard to see the coffin lowered into the ground. We heard the clergyman give what I later learned was the committal. We moved away to another part of the churchyard and when the funeral party had gone we went back to the grave to have another look, and stood and watched as workmen filled in the grave. I can't remember now whose funeral it was but I do know that it was a woman who was buried. At that time I don't think it really struck us that there was a body in the coffin; to us it was just another experience and it certainly didn't worry or sadden us at that time. On reflection, that woman has now lain in the churchyard at Barnfield for over a half a century. I wonder, did she ever know she had two inquisitive youngsters at her funeral? I don't think I went to another funeral until I was an adult and realised the sad truth of it all. At the school, the girls' playground and the school garden were separated from the churchyard by a fence which was about three feet high. When a funeral took place, play time or gardening lessons were cancelled, as people burying their loved ones didn't want a background of shouting and laughing from a crowd of school children.

If one continued along the lane which ran past the Kings Head and the football ground, one came to a five-barred gate which separated the end of the lane from farmland. Around Barnfield few arable crops were grown. Most of the farmland was either used for hay or grazing except for the hop gardens. Consequently we children were allowed to roam over almost any of the farms, provided we shut gates behind us and kept out of long grass which was ready for mowing. We often climbed over this gate at the end of the lane and wandered across the fields to where there was a fairly large pond, called the Stackyard Pond because at one time hay stacks had been made in an area close to the pond. At about the time that the Loch Ness monster was in the news, a certain old gentleman from the village attempted to drown himself in the Stackyard Pond, fortunately without success, as he lived for some years afterwards. However he became secretly known to us boys as The Stackyard Monster.

At this pond we used to play with boats. These boats were nothing very special, being made for us by some adults or in some cases by ourselves. The Stackyard Pond was in an open situation, and on a windy day boats would sail across the pond, on still days one could pull the boat across the pond by having a piece of string attached to it, then running round the margin of the pond. We spent many happy hours down there, not "Messing about in boats" but messing about with boats. There were quite a few reeds or rushes growing on one side of the pond. One day my boat sailed in among these and became stuck. I got myself a thin, whippy stick from a nearby hedge with which I hoped to free my boat from the rushes. When I got back to the pond I found that the stick was scarcely long enough to reach the boat so I stood on the side leaning forward, stretching out the stick in an attempt to move the boat away into clear water. As I thrashed about with the stick, the inevitable happened and I over-balanced and fell into the water. I believe that in places the Stackyard Pond was quite deep so it could have been quite dangerous, but it was deep enough even at that point for me to get my clothes thoroughly soaked. I was quickly hauled out by my friends but you don't have to be in water long to get saturated. I didn't really fancy explaining to mother why my clothes were very wet, but fortunately this happened early in the afternoon and I wasn't due home for tea until five o'clock. As none of us in those days had watches, we could always get away with being a bit late back. I spent the afternoon, after my soaking, running about. It is surprising what a little sun and wind will do. I daresay I was still a bit damp when I arrived home at twenty-past five, but neither mother or father seemed to notice anything. Mother just said, "You're a bit late," to which I replied, "Well we all are. We've been playing down over the fields and the time went faster than we thought." She didn't ask which fields we had been in or what we had been doing, and I didn't tell her. My clothing dried properly overnight and mother never did find out I had been in the water. I never did tell her either.

On May 12th each year, we used to have a day's holiday from school if it fell on a weekday, as this was Barnfield Fair Day. The fair was an ancient tradition and had been held for many years, back as far, I believe, as the early years of the 14th century. It was an animal fair, and on this day each year the village came to life as farmers congregated there from the surrounding villages. Some drove cows or sheep from nearby villages and others came from further afield in cattle lorries. Pigs also came, usually in some form of transport, as they are not great walkers. We were there, of course, and thought we were helping when running beside animals coming into the village. I don't suppose we were really but all the farmers seemed cheerful and good-tempered on fair day. It was a day out for them as well as us. All the animals were gathered together in pens in the football field, and at about eleven o'clock the auctioneer started selling. This was an interesting event. The bids were mixed with dry and witty comments from other farmers. In the land outside the field, various merchants set up stalls. They could be heard shouting to prospective customers how good and how cheap their wares were. We listened to them for quite some time. Many of the things they offered for sale did look attractive. I know when I went home at dinner time I would tell mother about these traders, what they had for sale and how much they were asking. I don't think she ever put her nose into the village on fair day and so never saw these salesmen, but she dismissed them out of hand as cheapjacks and I remember I was given more than one lecture never to buy from this sort of people. Even when I grew up as she was convinced that they would have the best of the bargain. She was probably right, too. There was no chance of our buying anything at that time as we didn't have any money anyway. The pubs had a good day because the farmers used to crowd the bars, drinking beer or spirits and treating each other. Many also called for pies and sandwiches. The more wealthy ones would pay for a cooked meal. The landlords and their helpers were kept very busy, but they obviously had a profitable day as the licensing hours used to be extended for such a special occasion.

After lunch was over the auction continued and the animals plus probably ducks, geese and chickens changed hands. When all was done, farmers stood talking to each other for a while, then gradually the animals were driven away or loaded into vans and lorries for the journeys back to the various farms. Usually by May 12th the football season, in those times, was over. It was just as well because on fair day the field received its annual manuring. After the departure of the farmers and their stock, the auctioneer and his clerk, the traders packed up their stalls and stowed away the unsold goods into vans, and they also drifted away. Soon the village was as quiet and empty as usual and another fair day had run its course.

Some of the shops such as the bakers and grocers had vans for doing deliveries to the farms and houses some distance from the village centre, but apart from those we didn't see many vans or lorries except on fair day, as the only others about were those coming into the village to deliver to the various shops, and they didn't seem to come very often. I do remember one van which used to come to one of the sweet shops about once a fortnight and was often parked outside when we went home from school. Why do I remember this van; well it was bright orange in colour, had "Brooke Bond" painted on the sides and above all it had solid rubber tyres.

Opponents of hunting, and animal rights groups seem very much to the fore nowadays, and much is said and written about the effect on children of seeing a fox torn to pieces by hounds, or how cruelly animals raised for meat are treated. I wonder whether some of these people have ever seen a duck pen or a chicken house after a visit from a fox. The result is much the same as when the fox is caught by hounds except that when a fox enters poultry houses he doesn't leave many alive. He kills for the sake of killing.

We didn't have very much fox hunting around Barnfield although there were occasional meets in nearby villages. I, personally can take fox hunting or leave it, but we as country boys learned to accept the deaths of animals as something which was part and parcel of country life, but I don't think it ever turned us into sadists or made us want to inflict pain and cruelty on animals or people. If one were to grow good crops, then certain creatures had to be controlled.

On some Saturday or Sunday mornings in autumn or winter time when the breeding season was over, a group of men would often get together to visit a farm with the intention of catching rabbits. I have gone with them on many occasions. Usually death came quickly to the rabbits. The men would start by fixing a net over every rabbit hole they could find, then a man would produce a ferret from a bag, and this would be placed at the entrance to one hole. On smelling rabbit, the ferret would make its way down the hole in search of its natural prey. The rabbits were soon disturbed and would run madly to another hole where they thought there was an exit only to find themselves entangled in the net pegged across the entrance. As soon as a rabbit was seen in a net, a man would make his way to it and extract if from the net. There were two ways of killing it. Some men would put two fingers under its chin and jerk its neck back suddenly, which broke its neck, and others would hold it up by its back legs and strike it a sharp blow across the back of the neck with the side of the hand, which had the same result. It was all over very quickly. There were usually some holes that had not been found and were not netted. Rabbits escaping from these were often shot by men standing in the area with guns waiting for this to happen. Rabbits were not killed for fun. They ate a lot of grass wanted by farmers. They also found their way into gardens and quickly devoured carrots, lettuce, greenstuff and the like. Rabbits that were caught were taken home and eaten or sold to the local butcher. To farm workers they were a welcome addition to the family's diet, as workers on a farm were poorly paid. If my memory serves me correctly, they earned in the early thirties, just thirty-one shillings and sixpence (£1.57½) a week, which meant it was hard to make ends meet. Out of that wage some had to pay house rent, which I think was one shilling and sixpence (7½p) a week, although some farmers were a little more generous and gave their workers their cottages rent-free. It has always been a mystery to me that farm workers, who produce the most essential item of all, namely food, are still and always have been less well paid than workers producing non-essential items. Perhaps the answer is that most farmers and farm workers are totally committed to their work. When did we last hear of farm workers going on strike?

Father always had a gun while he was at Beechwood, and various creatures were shot for various reasons. Pigeons, especially in winter time, could make short work of winter greens, so these were shot and eaten. Sometimes we had partridges and pheasants wandering about Beechwood. These too were shot from time to time, in order to provide us with a meal, but of course they were never killed during the breeding season. We also ate rabbits which father shot, as he didn't appreciate them in the kitchen garden. Other creatures that were shot were rooks, which stole eggs and also often killed and ate chicks and ducklings; jays that would quickly strip a row of peas; and bullfinches, which in spring were often to be seen stripping the buds from fruit bushes and trees. Grey squirrels were also a great nuisance on an estate like Beechwood. They would eat eggs and kill the young of chickens and many wild birds; they would eat the buds from various trees, thus spoiling the shape, and I have seen ripe plums taken from trees and torn to pieces so that they could get at the kernels, which they treated like nuts. Grey squirrels are not the dear little creatures that town dwellers think they are when they see them in trees in the urban parks. Squirrels, too, were shot, usually in winter when the trees were bare, as it is very difficult to see squirrels for more than a brief moment when trees are covered with foliage. We often heard them, as they do not like cats and kick up quite a fuss when one is around.

As I grew older, about twelve or thirteen, I used to go out with father and was instructed on how to use a gun. Much stress was placed on safety. I was told many times, "Never leave a cartridge in a gun when you have finished with it; never push through hedges or undergrowth, or climb a gate with a loaded gun; and never cock a gun before you see something to shoot at." I was always told to make sure there were no people about before firing, as well. Father wasn't a great one for paying attention to detail at times and he certainly was not a worrier, but he was always very, very careful when using a gun. Gradually I was allowed to go out on my own with the gun, and felt that I knew what I was doing. I used to shoot rabbits, grey squirrels, and sometimes I would wait within sight of the chicken run after they had been shut up, as this provided an opportunity to shoot rats when they appeared in search of corn that had been left on the ground in the run. I must say it never occurred to me then, that a gun with sawn-off barrels could be used as a weapon when robbing various premises. Growing crops was a battle between man and various animals. We only used the gun to make sure that we won, or to provide us with food.

Sometimes Bert and I would visit the local slaughter house and spend the afternoon watching the son of the local butcher, whom of course we knew, killing animals and cutting them up for sale in the shop. We were well aware that many animals kept on farms were being reared for meat, and we regarded the killing of them as a fairly natural process. I feel that nowadays some people, even those who eat meat, like to feel that you can have meat without killing animals, or perhaps they don't think about it at all. I have seen bullocks, pigs and sheep slaughtered, and it was, at least, done quickly and cleanly. I am not suggesting that the humane killer was always used in country districts as it should have been, for they seemed to prefer the old methods of killing which their ancestors had used, and government inspectors were not exactly thick on the ground in remote places. A bullock usually grazed in the field surrounding the slaughter house for a few days before being killed, then it would be driven inside and a rope tied round its neck. The rope was passed though a hole in the wall, almost at ground level, then along the wall on the outside and through a ring. The rope was then pulled until the animal's head was in contact with the ground and then secured. Bert and I used to sometimes pull on the rope to help get the animal where the butcher wanted it. When all was ready he either killed the animal with the humane killer, or a mark of dye was placed on the bullock's forehead and the butcher would then pick up the pole-axe, an axe-like tool with a steel spike on the back and a fairly long handle. He would swing this like a woodsman swinging a felling-axe and bring the spike down with great force on the dye mark. I never saw him miss. The spike penetrated the bullock's skull and it fell immediately.

I can well imagine that this method of killing could be painful in the hands of an inept workman, but the butcher I knew was a skilled man and did what he had to do quickly and cleanly. After the animal had been killed, it was pulled up by rope and pulley and suspended head down from a beam. Its throat was then cut in order to get rid of the blood. In the north of England, I believe the blood is saved for black pudding making, but in Sussex it always seemed to be washed down the drain. I never remember seeing black puddings in butchers' shops in that district. It was then skinned by making a slit right along the belly, then gradually peeling back the hide until it was completely removed. The hide was, of course, sent to a tannery to be turned into leather. The slaughterman then made a deeper cut in the belly and all the internal organs were removed. These, such as kidneys, liver, heart and intestines were washed in cold water, then placed in bowls ready for transporting back to the shop. There they were thoroughly cleaned before being offered for sale. The intestines, after thorough washing, would be used for sausage skins. The rest of the carcass of the bullock was divided into quarters, wrapped in mutton cloth and also taken back to the shop to be reduced still further to family joints.

At the shop they had a great section of an oak tree trunk which was used as a chopping and cutting block. It must have stood two feet six inches high and been something like three feet across. I remember seeing Mrs Forbes, the butcher's wife, scrubbing it at night after the shop had closed. When she had finished, its surface was left gleaming white like a deal-topped kitchen table.

At the slaughter house, I preferred it when pigs were killed with a humane killer and bled afterwards. Otherwise it meant that the pig had its throat cut and was released to run round the slaughter house with blood pouring from it until it collapsed. Apart from the cut with the knife, it would have felt little pain and it did lose blood very quickly. No doubt this is how pigs were killed for hundreds of years when many labourers kept a couple of their own in order to help feed the family. The carcass of the pig was placed in very hot, possibly boiling, water, then scrubbed with a very stiff scrubbing brush which removed the hair. It was then treated in much the same way as a bullock except that it was halved instead of quartered.

The Forbes had two sons who worked in the business.

Both were big strong fellows who seemed to have no difficulty in picking up the carcass of a pig, placing it across their shoulders and carrying it to the van. At the shop, the head was removed and the remainder cut into joints of meat. Mrs Forbes used some of the pigs' heads to make brawn. This was done, presumably, in her kitchen at the back of the shop. The resultant brawn was poured into basins to set. Although we didn't normally have our meat from Forbes, there being two butchers in the village, I was sometimes sent there to get sixpenny worth of brawn, which was then tipped from a basin, cut into pieces, weighed and wrapped. Very good it tasted, too.

I cannot remember sheep being killed at the Forbes' slaughter house although they must have been at some time or other. I have seen sheep killed at the other butchers in the village and usually there it was a case of cutting the throat of the animal rather than using the humane killer. Both butchers had some farmland of their own where bullocks were reared, and one of them, I believe, also had sheep. Pigs were probably bought from farmers in the district. The butcher we dealt with used to make pork sausages which had a reputation for taste and quality which went beyond Barnfield. I must say that I have never tasted better since.

As I have said, we boys took all this as a matter of course, and as it was going to happen anyway we felt we might as well go to see it. It certainly didn't make us feel cruel in the way we treated our own animals, kept as pets. In those days we used to keep the metal skewers which came out of joints of meat, as the butcher was prepared to buy these back again. Mother used to put them on one side until we had collected quite a bundle and then she would say, "You can take the skewers into Mr Fields on your way back to school!" I used to take them in and we were paid twopence a dozen. I was allowed to keep this money but not allowed to spend it; I had to take it home and put it in my money box. We always used to save newspapers for Mr Fields too. Meat was wrapped in a piece of white paper or greaseproof depending what it was, then wrapped in newspaper. We used newspaper for fire-lighting, but what we didn't need we used to take to the shop. We didn't get paid for that but would be given half a pound of sausages or a piece of pig's liver with a, "Thank you. Give that to your mother."

Another event in the Barnfield calendar to which we looked forward was the annual Horticultural Show. This took place either on August Bank Holiday Monday or the previous Saturday, but I cannot be sure which. I incline to the Saturday, as there was often an all-day cricket match on August Bank Holiday Monday. As we used to take produce across the cricket field to the show I think I would have remembered if cricket had been going on at the time. Of course the bank holiday in those days was the first Monday in August and not the last as it is now. The show was held in the village institute, and was organised by a local committee which consisted mainly of professional gardeners of whom my father was one. There were quite a few in the village, as in-between the wars anybody with a garden of any real size used to employ a gardener, or in many cases more than one.

Assuming the show was on a Saturday, a group met in the institute on the Friday evening and erected the tables in the main hall. The tables were neatly covered with white paper, then marking up was done. Marking up meant that the tables were labelled with the various classes and divided up leaving sufficient space for the number of entries. Naturally the entries had been made by the prospective exhibitors a day or two before so that the total number of entries was known. The room behind the stage, known as the parish room because that is where the parish council met, was also used, but was earmarked solely for table decorations. The stage was more or less reserved as an office, as from there the entry cards were given out to the exhibitors as they arrived on the Saturday morning and the prizes were presented there in the evening.

My main interest in the show was the children's wild flower section; a bunch of wild flowers in a vase. For an evening or two before, I used to walk a considerable distance through the fields and woodlands, along roadside verges, under hedgerows and on the banks of the rivers searching for as many different kinds of wild flowers as I could possibly find. The schedule never actually stated what the judges were looking for, but it seemed fairly obvious that in addition to a large and attractive bunch of wild flowers the number of varieties obtained would carry considerable weight when deciding the prize-winners. My interest, I must admit, was somewhat mercenary. I was interested in wild flowers and knew many by name, but the prizes for those times were good, being half a crown (12½p) for a first prize, one shilling and sixpence (7½p) for a second and one shilling (5p) for a third. I should think that the equivalent today of the first prize would be about £3.75 or £4, and there can't be many village shows where you would get that amount. When one takes into consideration the small amount of pocket money we had which I have mentioned elsewhere, these sums were like a small fortune to us.

For several years I won that half-crown, and it went into my money-box to be converted into National Savings Certificates when enough had been accumulated. Mother, who was a great one for savings, directed our finances such as they were.

My other interest in the show was to see how much my father would win. Father was generally held in the village to be a very good gardener, so his reputation was to a certain extent, at stake on show days. Once again I find that my recollections of show days are that they were bright and sunny (it must have rained sometimes when we were children so why can't we remember it?) and that as usual father would be about early in order to make his preparations. He would soon be busy around the gardens of Beechwood cutting roses, gladioli, sweet peas, annuals and perennials to be shown in the various classes. He always took more than he actually wanted to guard against accidents. The extra blooms were discarded in the hall. Some vegetables, like beetroot and carrots would have been dug the day before and washed, but cabbages, cauliflowers, lettuce, peas and beans were not cut or picked until the Saturday morning as he wanted them to be as fresh as possible. Tomatoes and cucumbers were also left until the morning of the show. One class father was always keen to win was that of a collection of four plates of fruit. We had plenty of fruit at Beechwood including apples, pears, plums, gooseberries, raspberries, loganberries, red, white and blackcurrants, cherries, peaches and nectarines. There was one place in the village where they had a vinery and a melon house. Being able to show a melon and a bunch of grapes as two items in the collection gave the gardener there a head start, so father was always keen to produce other fruit of such quality that it offset the fact that he had no grapes or melons. He managed a first in this class on a couple of occasions but had usually to be content with second. The produce was gradually assembled and placed in trug baskets ready for carrying across to the institute. Not only did we have to take the items father was showing, but vases and jars in which to place the flowers as nothing was provided. I always helped take the show items to the village and we would walk with two baskets apiece across the cricket field to the road, then east to the institute, as the cricket field gate was nearer to the institute than the two other gates that gave access to Beechwood. On arrival, greetings were exchanged with other people who were exhibiting. Besides the open classes where people employing gardeners exhibited (entries were always in the names of the employers) or anyone else that wished, there were also what were known as cottagers classes for people growing stuff, either in their own gardens or on allotments. Father didn't usually spend much time talking on these mornings but systematically moved round the hall with me in tow with a jug of water, setting up his exhibits, six vases of sweet peas here, three vases of roses there, a pair of cabbages on this table and two cauliflowers somewhere else or whatever was required by the schedule. This of course took some little while as exhibitors tried to make their entries look as attractive as possible. At something like 10.30 a.m. or eleven o'clock the hall was cleared so that judging could begin. The only other people allowed to remain were members of the committee who were acting as stewards. These gave the judges any assistance they required by answering any questions put to them and when the judges had made their decisions the stewards wrote the winners' names on the prize cards. How I was attracted by those brightly-coloured prize cards, red for first, blue for second and green for third. When the judging was completed everyone went off for lunch and the show opened to the public at 2 p.m. I believe there was an admission charge but exhibitors were allowed in free.

How I looked forward to the opening of the show. As soon as I got inside I was off to the wild flower section to see what I had got in the way of a prize, if anything, and rarely was I disappointed. After that it was round the show, still rather excited, to inspect the prize cards in the other classes hoping to find red cards with Miss Barrington's name written on them for this would mean success for father. In view of the fact that he had fewer glasshouses than they had at some other places, he usually did pretty well. The man who grew the melons usually ended up with the highest amount of prize money, something over four pounds. Miss Barrington usually won between three and four pounds which she didn't claim so this meant that father, who collected it on her behalf, was allowed to keep it. This was as good as an extra week's wages or more.

The table decorations in the parish room were always very attractive and much admired. There were a number of tables, all the same size, set out in the room, and on each table there was in the centre a large vase or bowl containing a flower arrangement. Standing at each corner of the table was a smaller vase or container in which was a smaller decoration similar to that in the middle. Sweet peas, roses, nasturtiums, stocks, larkspur and gypsophila were all freely used but not necessarily all in the same arrangement. Mixed sweet peas and gypsophila always made a most pleasant and attractive collection of vases. I believe the first prize for a decorated table was seven shillings and sixpence (37½p). Somewhere around five o'clock in the afternoon all gathered for the prize giving. There would be the chairman of the committee and one or two local dignitaries on the stage. Silence would be called for and the chairman would announce the name of the largest prize winner. His or her gardener would go up to the stage to receive the money from whoever was presenting the prizes. Having received the prize, the recipient would then return to the hall amidst loud applause. The children's prizes were presented last, probably to ensure that we knew our place in the order of things. When we arrived on the stage we were expected to pull our forelock on being presented with the prize. It was all fairly natural and the way we were brought up. I don't remember resenting it either then or since. Mind, we certainly did know our place in those days.

After the prize giving a few comments would be made on the standard of the exhibits and then thanks would be expressed to the people who had made the show possible. Finally everyone was told that they would be welcome at the following year's show. After that people would start to gather up their exhibits and remove them from the hall. Father was never one for taking much back home and would give away nearly everything he had shown. I often benefited as people who had just been given a plate of tomatoes and a couple of cauliflowers would express their thanks by giving me a few coppers. I sometimes collected as much as a shilling in this way to add to any prize money I had won. The baskets would then be filled with vases, plates, jars and the odd item father was taking home and we would set off for Beechwood. Father would leave me to put things away in the cupboard in the potting shed and he would return to the institute to help dismantle the trestle tables and put away everything that had been used. I would then take the prize money that father had collected home to mother.

As I mentioned earlier, we had an Early Rivers plum tree in our garden and as mother had bought it she always regarded this as hers. It was a roundish, blue plum and fruited about the end of July or early August, so the fruit was usually ripe at the time of the show. Mother liked to enter a plate of these and if she won a prize she was as excited as a schoolgirl. She was never one for showing herself off in public, and if she went to the show she never stayed for the prize giving if she won anything. It would be left to father to do the honours. In things of this kind he was as much an extrovert as mother was an introvert.

Two other events took place in some years: the visit of a fair or a circus. I am not sure but I think the fair came most years, and I suppose the circus put on a show two or three times during my childhood. There were two venues that were used for these events according to the season. There was at that time a field next to the Stag Hotel which ran parallel to the village street and behind some cottages which bordered the street. It was there that the circus

110

people put up their big tops and gave their shows. The fair sometimes took place in this field especially if it came in the early spring or autumn. The fair owners preferred the football field because it was bigger, and it was there that they went in summer time, but of course they could not have it in the football season.

The first we usually knew about a circus coming to the village was when we found a man or woman from the circus standing outside the school when we left in the afternoon, giving out leaflets on which were printed details of the coming event, the venue and the times of the performances. They usually stayed for a couple of days. On one of those days they put on a special and cheaper performance just for children. Looking back, it is surprising that there were enough children in the village to make up a large enough audience to warrant a special show. I suppose the circus was a fairly small affair really but to us in those days it must have seemed like Billy Smart's circus of today.

Although mother was always very careful with money, she was always prepared to hand over a few extra coppers for me to go to anything of this sort. She never wanted me to feel deprived compared with any other children. Really, in many ways I was luckier than some of the other children, but I can't say I appreciated the fact at that time. On reflection, I now know this to be the case. Anyway, all my friends and I seemed to go to the circus and there was great excitement in the period between knowing about its coming and the time of the actual performance. On the day of the show, the afternoon at school wouldn't go fast enough, but eventually, like every other afternoon, lessons ended and we were free to go. We dashed off home as quickly as possible, then off to the field by the Stag Hotel to wait for the circus people to open up, take our money and allow us inside. I know there were no chairs in the big top; we sat on forms or benches. As we chattered to each other time soon passed and 5 p.m. arrived when the show was to start. I can recall more of the excitement of anticipation than I can of the show. I know they had quite a lot of horses which trotted round and round the circus ring and were ridden by bare-backed riders in flashy costumes who jumped on and off the horses while they were moving. There were some who stood on the horses' backs and others who climbed on to each other's shoulders and balanced there as the horses went faster. It was all clever stuff to us. They also had a horse which counted by tapping his hoof on the floor, and another which danced in time with the music. Of course they had clowns and there was the usual tumbling about falling over each other and various other things, and the typical water throwing sessions in which the one you thought was going to get wet ducked at the last moment so that another got the soaking. There were trapeze and high wire acts. We watched these open-mouthed, fearing that someone would fall, but of course they never did. Dogs did various tricks and sea-lions balanced balls on the end of their snouts and also tossed them to each other. A lady, bravely to us, stood in front of a board while a man threw knives in her direction. When he had finished she was pretty well surrounded by knives embedded in the wood, and remarkably close to her. Seeing relief on our faces that she hadn't been injured he then repeated the performance using small axes instead of knives. These were probably no more dangerous, but they made a louder noise as they struck the wood. The whole performance lasted about an hour and a half and gave us something to talk about for days afterwards. As soon as we departed, the circus folk were back at work getting ready for the evening performance. It always struck us how quickly they came and went. One day the Stag Hotel field would be more or less empty and within a few hours the big top was erected together with other tents. Caravans were parked in various parts of the field and also vans which held some of the animals, and people seemed to be everywhere. A couple of days later all was gone and the field was as empty as before.

The fair's arrival was announced by posters in shop windows or on buildings and sometimes by an advertisement in one of the local papers, either the Sussex Express or the Kent and Sussex Courier. The fair people were very adept at erecting the various stalls and side-shows, and got everything ready in no time at all or it seemed that way. Like everyone else I always went to the fair, and although some of the boys were mad on it, it never created that much impression on me, and I certainly didn't find it as exciting as the circus. One good thing about it was that you didn't have to pay to go into the field, so if you had no money you could still wander around and watch what was going on.

Like the circus I suppose it seemed bigger and better than it really was. They had the usual roundabout with an assortment of horses and cockerels to sit on. It was driven by a steam engine and there was always music playing while it was in operation. When it stopped we could just hop aboard and take a seat. The men who collected the money would come round to each of us in turn while the roundabout was going. They appeared to be very daring, moving about from place to place and sometimes jumping off altogether and back on again as it turned. There were the usual types of side-shows such as coconut shies, a rifle range, hoopla, roll a penny, and another where one had to knock down tins with wet sponges, and of course, darts. The butcher's sons were great at the coconut shies. They flung the wooden balls with great power. I have seen them break the coconut in half as well as removing it from its cup. After doing that several times they became decidedly unpopular with the fair people. They preferred to refuse the money rather than keep giving coconuts away. There were prizes at many of the side-shows, usually ornaments like china cats and dogs, and also dolls and teddy bears. The ornaments were of no real value, being what mother described as cheap and nasty, and to which she would not give house room. Mother might have been somewhat shy and retiring but she certainly had definite opinions about things.

There were swing boats, half a dozen in a line where you sat with a partner and pulled on a rope. The more you pulled the higher went the swing boat. I went on these with a pal of mine a couple of times but I always felt rather sick and was glad to get off. This was rather strange, as the sea never affected me in this way, and I was never seasick. I can't say I ever became very fond of the swings. As young children, most of us were given a few coppers to spend at the fair. These usually went on roundabout rides at one penny a time, or on roll a penny where we hoped the penny rolled would settle in a square with a number on it. If it did we got back our own penny plus the number of pennies written in the square. Sometimes we were lucky and won a few extra pennies, but all too often the penny we rolled overlapped a line and we lost our money.

It is strange how one recalls various happenings in one's childhood. I went to the fair once with father when it was being held in the field by the Stag Hotel. I couldn't have been very old or I would have been with my friends. While we were there along came a man I did not know, with a great grin on his face, who shouted, "Hello, Syd, how's things?" Father said that things were very well and the man then gazed at me and enquired, "Is this your lad?" Father said, "Yes, this is the younger of the two - Bob." They talked together for a few minutes and during that time the man took out his wallet, extracted a note or possibly more than one, and handed the money to father. He then looked at me and said, "Here you are young Bob, go and enjoy yourself," and much to my surprise, he gave me half a crown. This was an unheard of amount of money to be given by someone all at one time, so I said, "Thank you very much," and slipped the coin into my pocket before he changed his mind. I can remember this incident as though it happened yesterday. Most of the money went home to be put in my money box. I found out by listening to the conversation between mother and father on our arrival home, who the man was. He was called Chris Collins and was fairly well known for getting drunk. At these times he spent more money than he should have done, then had to try to borrow money to see him through until his next pay day. Father lent him money several times and apparently always got it back when Chris was sober and in funds. Sometimes he paid back the money and a bit extra. I'm not sure whether I got the bit extra or whether he had started to drink again and was feeling generous when he gave me the half-crown. I got to know him quite well in the following years, but sad to say all was not well with him and eventually he committed suicide. Two or three people in the village committed suicide during my childhood days, and all to do, I believe, with heavy drinking.

As I grew older I liked the rifle range at the fair as well as anything and fancied myself as quite a good shot. It was on this stall that they gave some of the china ornaments as prizes. I knew it was no good taking any of these home as mother would not welcome them. I did take a small black and white china cat home on one occasion and it disappeared rather quickly into the dustbin. Like the circus, when the fair was over, everything was taken down at top speed, loaded on to lorries and the fair people and all their belongings were soon on their way to their next venue where everything would just as quickly be set up again.

Apart from the activities already mentioned, most of us walked quite a lot. Bert and I, if we had nothing else in particular to do, would go for a ramble. The village itself was surrounded by farmland and woodland, so we had considerable choice as to where we should wander. Sometimes it would be across Beechwood, on to Keith Rowland's property to the lane which ran near the river in the Dudwell Valley, then back on to more of Keith Rowland's land and up through Manor Wood and across a large field of rough grass and bracken known as Hillside Acres and on to Dukes Hill, then on to the top of the hill and left along a country land where there was the Church of England mission room. Just beyond it was a stile which gave access to more farmland called Woodmans and we would cross this and come out onto Dukes Hill again almost opposite Manor Wood and make our way back to the village by School Lane. At other times instead of going through Manor Wood we would turn right just beyond Keith Rowland's house, past the mill pond, then follow paths across his farmland running west and then north which would lead us back to the main road at Sadlers Hill three quarters of a mile west of the village. There were also farms to the north of the village on either side of the golf links, and these we wandered across at will, sometimes to the east and at other times to the west. Whichever way we chose to go we usually covered several miles before returning home.

During these walks we kept our eyes open and learned a considerable amount about nature. When it came to September and mushrooms appeared we knew that we should find some in one of the fields of Woodmans or in a field in front of a row of houses in Wood Lane which ran from opposite the Duke of Wellington, crossed the railway line, and continued to other villages beyond. There was no question as to whether they were mushrooms or not, as from an early age we could tell a mushroom from other sorts of fungi. We could also tell a swallow from a house martin and we knew that it was the swallow that nested in farm buildings and the house martin which stuck its nest of mud to house walls just below the eaves. In the same way we knew that the rat-like creatures to be seen in the river and on the river banks were in fact water voles, and we also easily recognised dragon flies; knew that although they looked fierce as they swept across a pond, they were in fact harmless. Why, I wonder, did they ever get the name of devil's darning needles? We learned that they laid their eggs in the water and that the larval form was a nymph which devoured all sorts of other creatures found in ponds.

At times we saw other creatures such as stoats and weasels; and hedgehogs were commonplace. Once I was out with the gun and strolled down on to the tennis court at Beechwood. From the southern end you could look down a bank some eight or nine feet high, into Seven Acres. By coming across the lawn one could get a shot at a rabbit in the field now and again. On this occasion there about half a dozen rabbits sitting still and gazing, apparently spellbound, at the antics of a weasel. Of course while he was gambolling about he was gradually getting closer to a rabbit. As weasels will take chicks and ducklings I was trying to make up my mind whether to shoot the weasel or a rabbit, when something, I know not what, disturbed them all and within seconds the field was empty.

Grass snakes were common enough and I have seen them on the move, basking in the sun, and swimming. Incidentally, they are much at home in the water and swim very well. From time to time father would dig the rubbery-shelled eggs out of the leaf heap which he made every year in order to rot down leaves which eventually were mixed into potting soil. These leaf heaps generate a fair amount of heat, enough to hatch the snakes' eggs.

Toads and frogs were common; we often found a sleepy old toad under the water tank in the greenhouse. We also knew that newts could often be found in the pond in the corner of the football field. Blackberries could be gathered on the Beechwood estate, as brambles formed part of the undergrowth in the copse on the far side of Drive Field, and there were more in the hedges that separated Drive Field and Seven Acres from the land of Ted and Sarah Bowman who farmed there, although their farm house was in School Lane at the other end of the village.

Butterflies always interested me and I learned the names of many of them early on and also soon was able to recognise the caterpillars and knew which food plants they were to be found on. Of course meadow butterflies were much more common, as fields then contained a variety of common wild flowers mixed with the grass, whereas nowadays most farms have meadows which have grass and very little else. In the gardens at Beechwood we had both buddleia and sedum spectabile, both of which attract butterflies in large numbers. They were also to be seen on the ripe pears where wasps had already damaged the fruit. Orange tip butterflies were very common in the orchard, as there among the grass were numerous ladysmock plants on which their caterpillars feed. I have not seen an orange tip butterfly for twenty years, and very few ladysmocks in that time. In those days we had wide verges to the roads, except in the village street, where many wild flowers grew, and these in their turn attracted different sorts of butterflies. Along the lane near the river, meadow sweet used to grow in profusion, and at dusk the air was heavy with its marvellous scent. I can smell it yet.

Yes, we had a pretty fair idea of what went on in the countryside and of course I learned much from father, who had been a countryman throughout his life. This knowledge of the countryside leads me to recall as amusing story of what happened in a Sussex village when the evacuees from London made their appearance early in the war. Not only the children but the teachers too came from London, and all

118

were absorbed into the local school and the classes were soon a mixture of town and country children. Londoners regarded the country children as pretty dull and not nearly as worldly wise as themselves. A teacher from London, at a particular Sussex school, one day drew a picture of a cow on the blackboard and said to a country boy, "What is that, George?" George replied, "I don't know, miss." The teacher went on, "You silly boy, you must know what it is." "Well, I don't, miss," insisted young George. The teacher glared at him and said, "I'll ask you again," and pointing to the drawing went on, "Now, what is that?" Once again George insisted that he did not know. The teacher, exasperated at what she considered the boy's stupidity, walked down the classroom, grabbed young George by the scruff of the neck and propelled him to the front of the room. Pushing his face against the drawing she screamed, "Now, you stupid boy, what is that?" George, also by this time, rather exasperated, replied, "I still don't know miss, but I'll have a guess. It looks a bit like a cross between a shorthorn and a Frisian." Silence followed this answer until the teacher said, "Hm. Perhaps you are right," obviously not having the faintest idea what either a shorthorn or a Frisian looked like.

I often didn't see too many of my friends for long on a Sunday, as several of them were in the church choir. Not being in the least musical I did not aspire to such heights, so I was often at home when they went to sing at matins and evensong, although most of us went to Sunday school together in the afternoon. Those who had become choir boys also had to go to choir practice on a Wednesday evening. I don't really know whether it was the church, the singing or the money that attracted them, but I heard quite a bit about twopence for a practice and the penny for a service which they received. They were also paid extra for singing at weddings and funerals. If a funeral took place in the week during term time they were not available, being at school. Mr Atkins, the school's headmaster, was the

119

organist and choir master, so there wasn't much nonsense among the choir boys. If the organ was needed in school time the reserve organist was called upon to play.

Barnfield also had a village band and at times feelers were put out for boys to join. Obviously if the band was going to survive through the years, boys had to be trained to eventually take the place of those who either died or retired. This again, was not my cup of tea, but two or three of my friends joined and were taught to play instruments such as saxophone, clarinet or cornet. This, of course meant that they had to attend boys' band practice and also practise at home before they were ready to play with the band at their various engagements. The man who was a bandmaster, when I first remember it, came from a very musical family and at least three of his sons played in the band.

Near the church was a fairly big house where lived a Miss Hannah Matthews, who used to have tennis parties from time to time. An invitation came one day, through the Misses Barrington, for me to act as a ball boy at one of these tennis parties. Bert was also involved and several other lads of more or less my own age. We had to be there for one o'clock in the afternoon of a burning Saturday in June. Play started almost as soon as we arrived, and apart from a break for tea, went on until about seven in the evening. We were given a drink of lemonade during the tea interval, but apart from that, we chased tennis balls and threw them to players as they required them for the rest of the time. At the end of play we helped put chairs, tables and various items away, which meant carrying them down steps into the cellar. For our afternoon and evening labour we were given sixpence (2½p). I got home somewhere around a quarter to eight and of course mother said to me, "You're late," and I told her that play had lasted till about seven and we had helped clear up. She then asked, "What did you have for tea?" "We didn't get any tea," I answered, "just a glass of lemonade." I think she began to get a bit suspicious, for the next question was, "How much did you get?" "A tanner," I replied. She looked at me, straight in the face and said, "Sixpence for all that time. You're sure you haven't spent any?" Hoping she would believe me I answered, "No, mum. That's all we got, sixpence. Bert will tell you it's right, as he got the same." "Right," said mother, her face red and angry, "that's it. That's the last time you go there as a ball boy. We're not that hard up. In future Miss Matthews can go somewhere else for her boys." That was the first and last time I went there, too. If I was ever invited again I never heard about it. As I mentioned, mother had firm opinions about some things.

After war broke out I joined the junior section of the A.R.P. We were rewarded in the first place with an armband on which the A.R.P. letters were printed. We used to go to various meetings where we had lectures on what to do in the case of bombing and how to deal with incendiary bombs. We also received some instruction in first aid, but I don't think I learned much more than I had in the scouts from Colonel Jenkinson. After a number of sessions learning first aid we had to go one evening to the British Legion hall in a nearby village, to take a test. When we arrived, there were various people lying around in different attitudes, each bearing a label stating what was wrong with them. A "casualty" was pointed out and it was your job then to render first aid. The examiner asked my name, ticked it off on a list, then pointed to a young lady of about eighteen. I went across the room to her, looked at her label, and what was I confronted with but "fractured ribs". Now in addition to having a prominent bust, this young lady was also the vicar's daughter. I was still under sixteen and found the situation quite embarrassing. Somehow or other I had to get a bandage round her ribs, but I found that her bust kept getting in the way. I must admit it was very attractive but I was frightened of touching it, as I thought she might be

121

offended as this was 1940, not 1980, when probably even a vicar's daughter might not have minded. Somehow or other I eventually managed to get a bandage round her, but the examiner was unimpressed and I don't believe he thought it was keeping anything in place. He was probably right. My thought was, "Why the hell can't the men have the broken ribs?" Added to this I had my leg pulled by my pal who had been there and seen it all. He said, "Now I know why you took the first aid course. So that you could feel the tits of the vicar's daughter."

We used to do duty one night a week at a garage near the cricket field where the A.R.P. had an office with a telephone. As a junior I only did evenings from 7 p.m. to 10 p.m. with one of the men. I got on well with the man I shared the duty with. He was a local grocer who was a very gentle sort of man and very religious. He used to tell me about his time in France during the 1914-18 war and how thankful he was that he had never had to use a bayonet, as he wasn't at all sure that he could have stuck it into another man. He was obviously not cut out to be a soldier, but joined up because he considered it was his duty, but I gather there was always an inner struggle between his duty to his country and his religious beliefs. He would probably have been more at home in the R.A.M.C. than in an infantry regiment.

After a year or so we had an observation point and a caravan in the cricket field, where I later did night duty with my father. When a red alert was on we were given this information by the telephone exchange operator. In the caravan were bunk beds. I slept on the top one and father had the lower one. On a shelf, level with the top bunk, was a telephone which was very near the bunk occupant's ear. It is surprising how soundly one can sleep when young, as I can recall several times when a red alert was phoned through in the night being shaken by my father with the

122

enquiry, "Aren't you going to answer that phone?" I don't think he was ever very comfortable with a telephone, and probably regarded it in much the same way as I look upon a computer today. Outside on a short pole we had a circular disc with numbers round the edge and a pointer mounted in the centre. In the caravan was a map of the area showing the same numbers as on the circular disc. During a raid, if we saw the flash of a bursting bomb we swung the arrow round to point towards the flash and then counted the seconds till we heard the report. We then checked which number the arrow rested on and dashed into the caravan where we looked up the number on the map. Allowing a mile for each second between the flash and the report, we could roughly decide where the bomb had fallen. We then used to ring the information through to headquarters at Battle. I eventually got a uniform when I was almost eighteen, but by the time I was given it, it was almost time to hand it in again and go and get my naval uniform.

Of course, dances were held fairly regularly in the village, mostly in the institute, but as I wasn't musical, dances didn't do much for me and I avoided them. Whist drives were a different matter, as I enjoyed playing cards and so went to these which were held quite regularly, again usually in the institute, but sometimes in a room at one of the local pubs I went for enjoyment, but some people, ladies in particular, went for the prizes and were not pleased when they didn't get them. There was one lady in particular from a nearby village who used to come to these whist drives accompanied by her daughter. They both regarded whist as a serious business. I well remember this lady taking me to task at the end of a particular hand when she considered that, as her partner I had played badly and so lost her several tricks. The other lady at the table disagreed, as she took the view that I was young and had to learn. All I had to do was keep quiet and let these two have a violent argument. Mind, I know whose side I was on. I never won a prize for whist, but I did collect a prize of three half-crown savings stamps, as at the end of one whist drive I happened to be sitting on a chair which had the message, "Down with Hitler," chalked on the underside of the seat. We all agreed with that.

CHAPTER SEVEN

Although as a family we were always well fed and adequately clothed, the comfort provided in our cottage did not compare with what most people enjoy today. We were no worse off than many people at that time, and better off than some. In summer time the cottage was lovely with trees and shrubs behind, farmland and the valley to the south and surrounded by a garden full of flowers. True, these same things were all there in winter, but with bare trees and the ground at times covered with snow it presented an entirely different picture. I have previously mentioned the new scullery with its bath, sink and copper which was built just before I started school. It was here on Mondays, always on Mondays in those times, that mother did the washing. Father was always about early, and on washing days he would be off to the shed across the garden to collect sticks and larger pieces of wood for the copper fire. The copper was filled with water, bucketful after bucketful from the cold tap over the sink, then the thin sticks and newspapers were used to get the fire started. Once it was going, larger pieces of wood were pushed in and so the water was heated. Although there was quite a fire beneath the copper it never seemed to warm the room much. Once the water boiled, mother pushed the washing into the copper along with soap powder. The sheets, pillow cases, clothes etc. were pushed well and truly under with a copper stick. The stick resembled a broom handle but was made of very white wood, or perhaps it had been bleached through hot water, soap suds and many wash days. Naturally, once things got going the windows were flung open to let out the steam, which soon shrouded the room. Personally I hated washing days particularly in winter, as when I went home at lunch time I knew there would be a cold dinner. There would be cold meat left from Sunday's roast, fried potatoes and a vegetable of some sort, possibly dried haricot beans, or runner beans which had been salted down in September. This was usually followed by cold apple tart and cold custard. In those days I was not too keen on meat when it was hot, and liked it less when it was cold. Salted runner beans bore no resemblance to the fresh ones we had in the summer. School would not have been very warm, nor the walk home, then the house would be cold with open windows and possibly an open door where mother had been in and out to the washing line in the garden. After the cold dinner, mother was soon back in the scullery, taking more washing from the copper which would then be rinsed in a galvanised bath containing cold water. Before I could escape back to school, there was usually a cry from the scullery of, "Bob, give me a hand with the mangling." The mangle was a huge piece of machinery which stood against the wall opposite the window. It had two wooden rollers about three feet long and eight or nine inches in diameter. The wheel on the side was made of iron and was, probably, a couple of feet in diameter. Attached to it was a wooden handle. It was my job to turn this handle while mother fed washing between the rollers. The mangle was certainly efficient, as water was squeezed out in what seemed vast quantities to drain away into yet another galvanised bath placed underneath. The washing eventually emerged from the other side of the rollers and fell into a shallow wooden box fixed there for that purpose. Sometimes things like sheets were folded and put through again. On top of the mangle was a large metal bar which operated a threaded shaft and by manipulating this the rollers could be set closer together or further apart. With cold water running into the bath, the room seemed to get colder and more miserable the longer one was in it, and I

126

was always glad when I could put my coat on and leave, as I knew that by the time I returned, all would have been cleared up. Although I didn't realise it at the time, it must have been far worse for mother, for she was in the scullery all morning and the best part of the afternoon and had all the washing to do, besides, if the weather was fine, running into the garden to hang it on the line and get it in again when it was dry. Should the day be wet, things were worse than ever, as this resulted in piles of wet washing being folded up and placed in baths and bowls to await the following day when it was hoped the weather would be better.

Up at the big house, Beechwood, father used to stoke the boiler in the cellar which heated the water for the central heating. The next cellar, through which the pipes ran, was only used to store a few garden chairs, and I have known, in very wet periods, when the washing was taken up there and hung on makeshift lines in order to get it dry.

Why did I go home to dinner? In those times it was usual for everyone to go home from school to dinner unless one came from very far away. Parents then didn't expect teachers to look after their children during the dinner time, and those who stayed at school at dinner time were unsupervised. To get to school I had to walk through part of the pleasure-grounds, the orchard and kitchen garden at Beechwood, then through a green garden door set in the hedge and across Long Meadow and the field belonging to the Stag Hotel, from there along the village street to the church and down School Lane. It was about three-quarters of a mile, and this was done four times a day. It was not an unreasonable distance to cover, and there was never any question of taking sandwiches and staying at school. Some of the children who came from the top of Dukes Hill round by the C. of E. mission room and from outlying farms did bring packed lunches. Mrs Atkins was kind enough to make cocoa for them to drink at dinner time. The milk for the cocoa was boiled on top of one of the classroom stoves and the charge was, if I remember correctly, a halfpenny a cup.

To return to our cottage there was only one room which was ever heated regularly and that was the kitchen or living room where the cooking range was situated. The fire in that went out at night. When father got up in a morning to light it the house was completely cold. Sticks would have been dried in the oven the evening before so there were always paper and dry wood ready at hand to light up in the morning. Beside the range stood a scuttle of coal with enough small pieces of coal to put on once the sticks were blazing nicely. All this had to be done before breakfast could be prepared. Mother was one who believed in a good breakfast to start the day. We always had something like bacon, egg and fried bread, or perhaps in summer time, fried tomatoes in place of the egg. This room would remain comfortably warm for the rest of the day, for it was here that the dinner was cooked for midday, and where water was boiled for any purpose for which it was required; making hot drinks, washing up and for washing ourselves. When we boys got up in a morning there would be hot water for us to wash in but it was still pretty chilly stripped off in the scullery. Father always washed with cold water at the kitchen sink, often stripped to the waist, although he did wait for the water to boil before he shaved, for which he always used an open razor. Father never seemed to feel the cold much; he never wore a vest, scarf or gloves and while I lived at home he never possessed an overcoat. He was only prepared to put on a raincoat if it was actually raining. I remember someone in the village saying to me once, "If you meet someone on a frosty night walking down the street like an express train, with his jacket flying open and a pipe stuck in his mouth, that will be your dad." This was a pretty fair description, as he always walked as though he hadn't more than a few minutes to live and was keen to get

128

somewhere while he had the chance.

When we came to sit in the kitchen or living room in the evenings we often didn't feel the benefit of the fire completely, as in front of it would be a clothes horse, on which the airing was being done. On Sundays we sometimes had a fire in the sitting room, which was delightfully warm and cosy. The walls and ceiling were covered with sheets of asbestos, and once the open fire was lit and burning brightly, this room warmed up quickly and retained its heat. Conversely, it was cool and pleasant on hot summer days. Of course, the fire in the living room had to be lit for hot water and cooking every day of the year, so on a sweltering summer's day we also had the dubious pleasure of a fire when we sat down to eat.

There was no electricity, so the old flat irons had to be heated for the weekly ironing. These were heated on top of the living room range and while mother was using one, one or two more were heating on the stove, so that as one began to cool, another was hot enough to use in its place.

Cooking and ironing were warm work in those circumstances in summer and I remember mother with a face as red as the setting sun as she went about these tasks. In my early days there was no mains electricity in the village and apart from those houses where they could afford to install and run a generating plant we all managed with oil lamps. Up at the big house at Beechwood they had electric light, but the plant wasn't sufficiently powerful for us to have it put on at the cottage. Near the garage was an engine room in which was stored several dozen two-gallon cans of the petrol used to feed the generator which was looked after by Bert's father. Even when electricity came to the village we were considered to be too far away and the expense of having it connected too great. So throughout my childhood we used lamps which of course burned paraffin and gave a poor light compared with electricity. The lamps had to be filled regularly, the wicks cut when they burned lopsidedly and the glass chimneys cleaned. We always kept a spare lamp glass in stock in case the one in the lamp cracked. This wasn't exactly a common occurrence but it did happen from time to time, perhaps when someone opened a door and a draught of cold air met the hot lamp glass. We would perhaps go for months without mishap, then two or three would break in a short space of time. Once we had three break in a single week, which didn't make mother very happy, as they cost sixpence ha'penny each, and one and sevenpence ha'penny in a week for lamp glasses she considered a bit much, a bit too much.

The only room in which we had a carpet was the sitting room, the other rooms being covered with linoleum with odd rugs scattered here and there. In the sitting room we had a suite of a sofa, two armchairs, and four dining chairs, all covered in green velvet. This, together with a sideboard and an oak gate-leg table made the room quite attractive. The suite was French-made and had been bought new when my parents married in 1915. Years later when I was clearing out the home I came across a receipt for furniture they had purchased at that time. There on the bill was the green suite at £6.10s. (£6.50) the lot. The dining chairs my brother has still, although they have been re-covered.

Going to bed in winter time was something of an experience. We had candles to light our way, then we had to undress in a cold bedroom. To warm the bed, when I was small, I had a firebrick which had been in the oven for some hours before I went to bed. It was taken out, wrapped in a cover and placed in the bed, which certainly warmed the bed and made it more pleasant to get into. I found, however, that as the brick cooled down so did I, so when I was a bit older I dispensed with the brick and dived into the cold bed. I soon warmed up and found that the bed remained warm until I got out in the morning. Another disadvantage of the brick was that when one turned over in the night, as likely as not one's feet came into contact with it, and, like most bricks, it was hard, and didn't do your toes very much good. There was a bedside rug to get out onto in the morning but I needed to be sure to get my socks on before I stepped off the mat because the linoleum in unheated rooms got very cold. It was rather like standing outside on cement with bare feet.

There was always something to do and my parents always seemed to be busy. Mother was never one to buy anything if we could provide it ourselves. Neither was she ever prepared to waste anything if it could be put to good use. I dread to think what she would have thought of convenience foods had she ever seen them. All sorts of fruit and vegetables were used in various ways in order to avoid waste. Cauliflower, onions and marrows were turned into piccalilli, and tomatoes, both red and green were made into chutney. Haricot beans and spare peas were dried and stored. They were then soaked overnight before use in winter time, then cooked in the usual way. Lots of fruit was available. Plums, damsons, cherries, rhubarb, strawberries, gooseberries, raspberries and loganberries were all turned into jam. Mother used to make jam for the Misses Barrington. They used to tell her what was wanted, then it was left to mother. When it was done, Miss Emma would call at the cottage and mother would inform her how much the sugar had cost. This would be reimbursed and there was something extra for mother's time and trouble. I don't imagine she ever made much out of it as it was our coal that was being used to fuel the range. I never understood why mother was asked to make the jam, as the Barringtons kept a cook and two other maids, all of whom lived in.

Actually, money had to be saved each week at home and put away, because our coal was delivered in bulk in summer time. We had two and a half tons every summer when it was a bit cheaper than the winter prices, but this, though beneficial, was not the real reason for the bulk order. It was difficult to get near our cottage by motor transport. Coal merchants were not prepared to deliver weekly and carry sacks of coal down through the gardens to our cottage, so delivery was made in the summer when Drive Field was firm and dry, and a motor lorry was not likely to get bogged down as it may well have done in winter time. The lorry was driven off the drive, down across the field and through the gate dividing Drive Field from Seven Acres. Our garden gate opened into Seven Acres, and it was through this gate that the fifty sacks of coal were carried and the contents of each dumped in our coal shed. The cost between the wars was, I believe, £2.10s (£2.50) per ton. This coal, together with the logs we burned, saw us through the year. I can hear mother now saying in about September of each year, "Well, I've got the coal money together." I never really took much notice of it or thought much about it at the time but I daresay it would have had a considerable impact on us if she had said that she hadn't got the coal money. To her it was an achievement but to me it was just normal.

In September, pounds of spare runner beans were washed, stringed, sliced and packed into salt in earthenware crocks for winter use. I never cared for them very much, but I still had to eat them. Mother's saying was, "It is good food. Eat it or go without." We ate it. It wasn't much good saying, "I don't like it," in our house. The beans were placed in a crock, then a layer of salt was put on top, then more beans and more salt until the crock was full. We kept chickens and far more eggs were laid in summer than in winter, and when they were plentiful, so many each week were put into crocks of isinglass, which would preserve them for winter cooking. After hens had ceased to lay to any extent, they were killed and eaten. As they were old, they were boiled, or sometimes boiled and roasted afterwards. Very small potatoes, which mother referred to as chats (this may be a north country term) were not wasted either. These were boiled and mashed, then mixed with chicken meal and fed warm to the poultry on winter mornings.

We also kept bees. Father looked after some that were hived in the gardens of Beechwood and belonged to Miss Barrington. We had two or three hives of our own in the cottage garden. Father had had experience of bees from the time he was a boy and managed the hives quite capably. Every so often he opened up the hives to check that all was well, or to add extra sections where the bees stored honey. He never bothered much about getting stung, as that sort of thing didn't normally worry him. He did, however, wear a hat and veil, and used a smoker when the honey was removed in the autumn, as the bees, quite naturally, did not appreciate or agree with this operation and often made their views very clear. On one occasion he donned hat and veil and went off to remove the honey. We didn't see or hear anything of him for a while, then mother caught sight of him making his way through the laurels and yews at the back of the house. She said, "I don't know what your father is doing, but he's creeping about in the bushes." We found out later what he was doing. He was beating a retreat. Apparently, though he hadn't noticed it, there was a small hole in his veil. The bees soon discovered it and soon were inside the veil and punishing him rather badly. He eventually left the bushes and made his way indoors to remove hat and veil and get rid of the bees still inside. He had been stung quite badly on the face, head and neck and within hours his face was very badly swollen. This didn't deter him, as with the hole in the veil mended, he returned to battle with the bees and secured the honey.

There was another time when the bees at Beechwood

were very angry and got after both father and Charlie Barnes, a young fellow who worked with father in the gardens. The first I knew of it was one dinner time when I was with Ken Edwards coming home from school. Suddenly he said to me, "Coo, doesn't that fellow look like Charlie Barnes?" He did look like him because it was Charlie, but with a badly swollen face. He was on his way to his home in the village street for lunch. As soon as Ken drew my attention to him I realised what had happened and expected to see father looking as bad when I reached home. He, however, wasn't too bad and it seems that Charlie had suffered most.

The hives in our garden stood beside the path which ran in front of the sitting room window towards the garden gate, but they actually faced Seven Acres. This was a bit unfortunate really, as the hawthorn hedge which separated our garden from Seven Acres was right in the bees' flight path and in the end had to be cut late in the evening when the bees had returned to the hives. I was a bit unlucky with that boundary, as I was once standing on a pair of steps clipping the hedge and suddenly got stung several times, then realised I was in the way of bees returning to the hive. They will not turn aside to go round one.

In one corner of the garden the hedge stopped about five feet short of the angle and a section of iron fencing was fixed in the gap. This we often used as a stile if we wanted to get into Seven Acres. When I was very small I once spent some time playing on this fence, and a few days later developed ringworm on my legs. The cattle in Seven Acres had ringworm, and they had been rubbing themselves against the fence before I climbed on to it. The trouble, I recall, was diagnosed by the butcher's delivery man and treated by the local chemist.

Mother always made her own cakes. I can scarcely

remember ever seeing bought cake in the house during my childhood. She used to ring the changes, sometimes making madeira or sultana cakes, whilst at others she produced cherry or mixed fruit cakes. She also used to make tarts with either jam or lemon curd, mince pies, ground rice cheese cakes and eccles cakes. The lemon curd was also made at home. It was all good stuff, as mother was pretty useful as a cook and could cope with most things. The only thing I can't remember her making is bread, and that was always delivered from one of the local bakers, although we were some way off the main road.

As well as growing flowers for sale, father used to make sprays and wreaths for funerals. People in the village got to know that he was quite a good hand at this sort of thing and it was, of course, much cheaper getting father to make a wreath than getting one from a florist in the nearest town where there happened to be a florist's shop. In winter time when flowers were short, I have known him go to Heathfield or even Tunbridge Wells to buy flowers and even then he could make up a wreath cheaper than people could get one from a shop. When my parents went shopping to Tunbridge Wells, father would buy a stock of various types of wires used for wreath making and so he was always prepared if his services were required. I have known him make up the wire frames which were used as the base for wreath making, but eventually he came to an arrangement with the verger at the church. When flowers on graves were dead and removed by the verger he would save the wire frames and pass them back to father. No doubt the verger got a few shillings out of it.

The moss which was used to pack the frames was obtained from Drive Field. There was an area where it grew quite thickly. Father would go and rake out as much as he needed at any one time. Incidentally, the first indication we often had of a death in the parish was the tolling of the

135

church bell, which used to ring every half minute or so over a period of an hour. There was, at times, great speculation as to who might have died. Various names of people who had been ill were put forward and it really became a topic of conversation until the news broke and someone was named.

Once, when a very tall man, he must have been six feet six inches, died, father was asked to make a cross which would exactly fit the coffin. He had to go to see one of the local builders who also acted as undertaker, to find out the size of the coffin. There was none of this large, medium or small then, as every one was individually made. Father then made up the frame to the correct size, packed it with moss and gradually worked in the foliage and flowers. When it was done it really did look attractive, but as it needed to be handled carefully, it took two men to deliver it to the house concerned.

Father was quite friendly with another gardener called Bill Talbot, who had a son. When the son's father-in-law died, Bill came to see father to see if he would line the grave. It was spring time and the family wanted it done with violets and primroses. Bill said he would help father, and they went off together picking huge bunches of primroses which grew in profusion in the Barnfield area. Added to these were cultivated violets which father grew in a cold frame. The funeral was to be in a nearby village, so all these flowers plus a roll of wire netting and a number of wooden pegs had to be taken several miles. I don't know how they got all they required to the right place, but get it there they did. The wire netting was pegged to the sides of the grave and the stems of the flowers were worked through the holes in the netting until it was all covered. As the ends and sides of the grave covered about one hundred square feet, it took an awful lot of flowers to complete the lining. I had never heard before of anyone having a grave lined and

I've never known anyone have it done since. To me it seemed a pity to bury all those flowers as well as the coffin.

Father was usually kept busy in the fortnight before Christmas, as he would then have orders for two or three dozen holly wreaths. These were made up after working hours, and as there was no light in the potting shed, the wreaths had to be made at home. For several days, therefore, every available surface in the scullery seemed to be covered with wire frames, holly and moss, and florist's wire. Gradually order was restored as the wreaths were completed and taken away to be placed on nails in the potting shed until they could be delivered. This, of course, provided a useful bonus for the family exchequer.

Strangely enough, father didn't really hold with flowers for funerals and used to say, "I think it's a daft idea, but I'm glad they do it." He also used to say, "I've worked with flowers all my life, but I certainly don't want any when I'm dead and cannot see them." He must have felt quite strongly about this matter, as he had a clause put in his will to say he wanted no flowers at his funeral.

One other time of the year when everyone on the outdoor staff at Beechwood was busy, was during the week or so in summer before the grounds were opened to the public. They were opened in aid of some nursing charity, I believe, but I am no longer sure about it. Certainly the young Miss Barrington was interested in nursing, as she had been a nurse for a period during the first world war. There was no admission charge, so money must have been raised by collection. Miss Barrington would discuss with father which Sunday would be most suitable for this event, when the grounds would be looking their best. Once a date had been arranged, notices were displayed in shop windows in the village and an announcement would be printed in the parish magazine. Father always liked the place to look good but an extra effort was put in on this ocasion so that everything was as attractive as possible. Consequently father and the other men put in quite a lot of overtime (all unpaid in those days) making sure that everything was neat and tidy. The Barnfield band was invited and its members settled themselves in the shade of trees on the lawn above the iris garden and played for several hours with breaks now and again for refreshment. At some time during the afternoon or early evening one was bound to hear the strains of "Sussex by the Sea" echoing around Beechwood. If Long Meadow had been mown and cattle were grazing in it, Bert and I would stand by the green door which gave access to the garden, not to greet people, but of course we knew practically everyone who came, but to make sure that the door wasn't left open so that bullocks could make their way into the garden, because cattle always seem to think that grass is greener on the other side. In those days there was practically no vandalism, and supervision in the grounds was very low key. Father would, however, wander round a time or two during the afternoon just to see that everything was all right. I never recall hearing of any damage being done on open days, or of father having to speak to anyone for misbehaving. If Cocoza heard about this event, and he usually did, he would bring his ice-cream van into the cricket field and oblige prospective customers.

Although both mother and father worked hard, they relaxed at times and we had some entertainment in the home. We had a gramophone in a wooden cabinet and naturally, at that time, it was one which needed winding up before each record was played. An electric one would have been no use to us anyway. It played the old, easily broken, 78 r.p.m. records and the music was produced by using gramophone needles, bought in tins of fifty or a hundred, which had to be changed after playing a few records. The cabinet had a lid which, when lifted, could be secured with a metal stay. This lid gave access to the turntable. In front were two small doors and these, when opened, revealed the loudspeaker. Mother's favourites were, "The Isle of Capri", "When it's Springtime in the Rockies", and "My Little Grey Home in the West". I still have one of these old records of a baritone called Fraser Gange singing "Lassie o'Mine" and "Achal by the Sea". For years, until it disintegrated, I had the original sleeve marked with the price of one shilling and sixpence (7½p).

Sometime in the thirties it was decided that we should have a radio, but unfortunately mother decided to let the gramophone go in part exchange. Soon after the decision had been made, along came a man with a radio, a Cossar, I believe, and he proceeded to fix up an aerial and fit a dry H.T. battery into the back of the set. The set was placed on a table under the window in the living room, and the aerial came into the room through a hold drilled in the window frame. Two other wires protruding from the back of the set were fixed to an L.T., or wet battery, which stood on the window sill. When all this had been done, the radio actually worked when switched on. At that time it was called a wireless, and as a boy I wondered why, as the back seemed to be full of valves and wires. Anyway, we had our wireless, and it was listened to a good deal. I had to learn to sit still and keep quiet when news bulletins were being broadcast.

My chief interest in the programmes at that time was listening to sport. On Saturday afternoons in winter they broadcast a commentary on a league football match, and I often listened to that if Barnfield were not playing at home. We then got the football results which previously we had had to wait for until we got the paper on a Sunday morning. There were also broadcasts of the tennis from Wimbledon, but better still, commentaries on the test matches. They were not continuous as they are now, but one could keep in touch with what was going on. Will I ever forget the news

139

from The Oval in August 1938 when Len Hutton got his 364 and beat Bradman's record. The England score at that time stood at 770 for 6 wickets and I think Howard Marshall was broadcasting. Little did I realise at that time that this was to be the last test match against Australia until a world war had been fought and won.

Mother was quite keen on horse racing on the flat. She used to have a bet on some of the more important races of the year and listen to the broadcasts on the wireless. What excitement I found one day when I returned from school to learn that she had backed Midday Sun in the Derby, which had come in first and she had won several pounds.

The wet batteries, or accumulators, as they were often called had to be recharged, so we had two of these, one in use and one at the cycle shop being recharged. Each week, usually on a Friday evening, when I went that way with flowers, I took one battery and dropped it off at the cycle shop, and collected the other on my way back home. The charge for this was sixpence each week. The dry batteries used to last three or four months according to how much the wireless was used. These were quite expensive, being twelve or thirteen shillings each.

We always had pets of some sort; not in great numbers, but always one or two. My brother had a tortoise at one time, but I really can't remember very much about it. He also kept bantams at one time. He had bought himself these, and I think he intended to breed from them with the intention of selling the chicks. All went well to start with, until I became involved. Bantam cocks can sometimes be very aggressive, not only to other bantams, but to human beings, and Ted's bantam cock picked on me. I must have been quite young at the time, as I was riding a little tricycle along the path beneath the sitting room window. It must have been a Saturday afternoon in late September or early

140

October, as father was planting wallflowers. As I rode along the path, this bantam cock seemed to appear from nowhere and flew straight at my face, obviously with evil intent. I don't think I even shouted, but father, who saw what was happening, grabbed the bantam and wrung its neck on the spot. I don't think Ted was too pleased when he knew what had happened. He wasn't the only one. I wasn't exactly thrilled when it happened, and neither was father.

We also had a rabbit, a grey chinchilla, which had a run under the apple tree in the garden. We used to wander round Beechwood to collect wild parsley, commonly known in the country as rabbits' meat, and dandelions on which to feed him. When these were not available he had bran and the occasional carrot or cabbage. He chewed his way through the wire netting of his run several times, and we found him in the garden where he had found more interesting things to eat, and consequently incurred mother's displeasure. The wire netting was repaired several times, but there came a day when we found it had been bitten through once again, and Billy as we called him, was nowhere to be found. We decided that was the last we should ever see of Billy, but much to our surprise, after three or four days, he turned up at his hutch again. I keep referring to "him", but I don't think that anyone had taken too much notice of part of "him", because a few weeks later "he" produced a litter of half-wild baby rabbits, having obviously mated with a wild buck during his absence from home. Even when "he" became she, we called it Billy.

My favourites, however, were the cats. I was always very fond of cats and still am. When my parents moved to Beechwood from Southcourt, they took a cat, Pincher, with them. I heard that he returned to Southcourt several times after they moved, but I don't know what happened to him in the end. It was about this time that they obtained a kitten from someone who lived at Sadlers Hill. This kitten came

141

into the world about the same time as me and was part of the family from the time I can first remember. She was completely black. We called her Sooty, and she was my constant companion for my first ten years. She was a great hunter and would come home with rats, mice, rabbits, various birds and anything else she could lay her claws on. She appeared on one occasion with a fully grown cuckoo, and on another she returned home with her teeth firmly fixed into the neck of a grass snake, the body of which was stretched between Sooty's legs and protruded behind her. Mother disliked snakes and Sooty was told that that was the first and last time she need bring one home. About twice a year she produced kittens. These turned up in all sorts of odd places, such as in a cellar of the big house at Beechwood, in a frame in a box of seedlings (not to father's liking), in the farm buildings in Long Meadow and under our pile of firewood in the garden. We kept a tabby-coloured one, which very originally, we called Tabby. Tabby grew into a lovely cat, very affectionate and mother thought the world of him. Sometimes he would disappear for four or five days at a time, and just as suddenly turn up again when we had reached the stage of not expecting to see him again. Unfortunately he caught cat 'flu when he was four or five and didn't survive.

When we had kittens I adored them, and when old enough I went round asking people if they would like a kitten. I found homes for quite a few, but there were times, sad for me, when no one wanted them and father had to destroy them. When I was ten we had one kitten, a little black one, left and as it was a female, no one wanted it. Father kept saying she would have to go but before he got round to it, Sooty failed to come home. She had been missing a while when a foul smell began to creep across the iris garden. We didn't connect the smell with Sooty, but father thought perhaps it was a dead rabbit or something and made a search of the iris garden and the rhododendrons and laurels in the surrounding area without result. It was summer time and the smell didn't improve, but one evening Bert's sister came down home for something and announced she had seen Sooty asleep in the iris garden. We all went dashing up the path to see. In the angle where a fence with a honeysuckle trailing along it joined the steps going into the iris garden, lay the old cat, dead of course. She just seemed to have curled up and died. In view of the smell, father decided he would bury her in the iris garden, by moonlight. The next day the smell had disappeared. Sorry as we were to see Sooty go, this meant that we could keep the kitten, and as she was black, she too became Sooty.

I spent hours with this one and was very fond of her. She, in her turn, produced kittens, usually under the wood pile, but on a couple of occasions, under one of the bee hives. It stood on bricks and she had squeezed underneath. The kittens had been born there. It was not always easy to find the kittens either, for if she thought any of us was looking she went a round-about way back to her family. When she was about two, she also had cat 'flu, which had become epidemic in the village and lots of cats had died. She lay in a box, lined with hay, in the house porch for the best part of a week and refused to eat. Eventually after we had had chicken, I put some on a saucer and took it out to her. She raised her head, sniffed, then slowly got up from her box and started to eat the chicken. She made rapid progress after that, and within three or four days she seemed completely back to normal except that she still looked rather thin.

When the next lot of kittens arrived, I traced them to a hollow under the wood heap. With difficulty I got them out, one by one and transferred them to the box in the house porch, only to find hours later, that they had all gone again. It was just as though she had thought, "Why don't you mind your own business." They were back under the wood pile. I had quite a battle with her over them, for as fast as I removed them from the wood pile, she took them back again. In the end she decided to leave them in the box. I remember that particular lot very well; there were four, two black, one tabby and one a sort of stripey grey. I found that when I picked them up or stroked them, Sooty would promptly wash them, so, childlike I suppose, I used to wait until she had washed them all and then pick them up one by one, then watch her carry out the operation all over again. I was the one who got tired first. As the kittens grew older, opened their eyes, and left the box, I found that I could persuade them to follow me round the garden. Several times I was seen marching along the garden path followed by four kittens in line astern, each with its tail pointing to heaven.

Sooty was a bit of a character. Often at dinner time she would come home to see what was on offer, and if she didn't fancy it she would promptly disappear to catch something more to her liking. In the rabbit breeding season, she would locate a nest and catch the young rabbits one by one, then sit over the hole for a day or two more to make sure she hadn't missed any. At Beechwood they had a dog, a saluki called Raffie, who had a kennel on the concrete near the garage. Bert's father used to let him out each morning when he went to work. He immediately dashed down through the gardens, down the path to our cottage and looked for Sooty, who, if found, would shin up the nearest tree and stay there until Raffie had gone. What a different story it was though when kittens arrived. I have seen Raffie appear the morning after the kittens were born, but he would find a very different cat. No trees this time, as she would turn on him, big as he was, and the next minute Raffie would be tearing back up the same path he had just come down, with the cat not far behind and full of evil intention. We didn't see the dog again until the kittens had gone. Then the game would be resumed and she would oblige him by climbing a tree once more.

I don't think Sooty normally ever went away from the Beechwood estate. She once developed some irritation under her chin which she scratched until she had removed all the fur from quite an area of her throat. Vet fees were not for us if they could possibly be avoided, but a van belonging to the People's Dispensary for Sick Animals used to come to the village once or twice a week, so I caught Sooty, put her into a rush bag and fixed a skewer through the top to stop her getting out, and carted her off to the man who came with the van. He had a look at her and smeared the bald area with a yellow ointment resembling acriflavine and then put her back in the bag. I carried her through the field of the Stag Hotel and let her go in the beech plantation at the entrance to Long Meadow. Next time I saw her all the ointment had gone, apparently washed off. Perhaps it worked from inside because the irritation seemed to disappear and her throat was soon covered with fur again.

We never kept the cats in at night, but I don't really know why. The last thing father did at night before going to bed was to put the cat out. Sooty was none too enthusiastic about this, especially in winter. On cold nights she used to try to find some more or less inaccessible place, especially towards bed time. One of her favourite hideouts was under the kitchen range. Now mother, when she cleaned the range with emery paper and black lead, used to finish the job by going over the floor under the range and the area just in front, which we called the hearth, with whitening. When Sooty was finally persuaded to leave this spot, sometimes with the aid of a walking stick, she emerged as a black and white cat, white on the side on which she had been lying. When next one saw her she had returned to her normal colouring, obviously having licked off the whitening powder.

Mother and father always, even on the coldest nights, slept with their bedroom window open, and beneath the window, the branches of a plum tree were secured to the wall. The cat had observed this and developed the habit of returning after being put out at night, climbing the plum tree and re-entering the house through the bedroom window. It was never a very productive plum tree, so father observed, "Right, I'll soon stop that little game of hers," and immediately went for a ladder and a saw and removed the branch under the window. That night, not being deterred, Sooty climbed the plum tree in the dark to where the branch had been removed, and from there then jumped across on to the sloping sill and came in as before through the window. As suddenly as she had started coming back at night she stopped and I don't think she ever did it again in the dark. She didn't come to much harm, as in the farm buildings in Long Meadow there were four mangers filled with hay. She burrowed her way to the bottom of one of these and slept in it completely surrounded by hay, so what with the hay and a thick fur coat, she must have been warm. Mind, she hadn't exactly forgotten that window, for once, when she had kittens she took them up the plum tree one at a time and jumped that gap with a kitten in her mouth and finally deposited all four kittens on mother's bed. When they were discovered, they departed rather faster then they had arrived. Mother didn't approve of cats on her bed. On day I was in the room that had been my brother's bedroom before he went away from home, and the cat realising this soon joined me. She jumped upon the sill and sat by the open window purring away, hoping to attract my attention. I went across and stroked her. In her ecstasy she rolled over on her back and disappeared out of the window. There must have been a drop of at least fifteen feet, but she landed on all four paws and just strolled away completely unconcerned. She never even looked up at me.

There came a day when Sooty failed to put in an

appearance at breakfast time as she usually did. This was strange, as she never went away as Tabby had done. Three days passed and still she didn't return, but on the fourth she staggered round to the cottage looking thin and dragging behind her a wooden peg attached to a rabbit wire. When father saw this rabbit snare he was very angry, as he never allowed rabbit wires to be used at Beechwood because of the cats, and as we had never known the cat leave the estate, he suspected that someone was coming on to Beechwood to snare rabbits without permission. In other words, we had been visited by poachers. Sooty had put her head through the wire noose, probably in the dark, but fortunately she got one front leg through as well. When the noose tightened, this meant that it did not strangle her as it was not completely round her neck. However, she was stuck, as the wire was attached to the wooden peg which had been driven into the ground. Of course, the more she pulled the more the wire cut into her. She had obviously put up a struggle and at last succeeded in pulling the peg from the ground, but the wire had cut into her quite badly. After the wire had been removed, mother treated her with germolene, which seemed to do the trick, as the wound healed quickly. When her fur grew over the cut it came white, and so for the rest of her life she had a thin line of white hairs to mark where the rabbit wire had been.

When I went to school at Tonbridge I had to cycle to the railway station in order to catch the train to that town. Sooty got into the habit of going with me as far as the inner drive gate, which was by the forecourt of the big house. When I came home at night she would be waiting in the same place, and while I rode my cycle up to the garage and down through the gardens to our cottage, she would make her way down across the lawn in front of the big house where, as children, we were never allowed to go, and she would be home by the time I arrived. This happened time and time again while I was at school and also during the short period I worked before joining the navy.

I did my initial training at H.M.S. Royal Arthur, which was in fact Butlin's Holiday Camp at Skegness. Whilst there I had a letter from mother in which she said, among other things, that the cat didn't seem very well. At the end of five weeks I was drafted to London to undertake a trade course, and was given a short weekend leave before it started. I went home and the cat seemed as fussy as ever. There appeared to be nothing wrong with her. When I returned to London on the Sunday evening, my parents came across to the village to see me off on the bus to the station, and the cat followed us through the gardens. At the green door leading into Long Meadow I bent down to stroke her and she stayed in the garden while we went across the field. That was the last time they saw Sooty alive. Father found her a day or two later curled up under a yew tree opposite the larder window of the cottage. I fancy, she took, was a war casualty.

CHAPTER EIGHT

Christmas in Barnfield was, as everywhere else in the country, the most exciting time of the year for us children, perhaps more so than it is today because it was only then that we had a real present.

Before the presents, though, there were the preparations which started at home with mother making Christmas puddings and mincemeat. Ingredients for these had to be prepared because we did not buy seedless raisins and packeted peel, if they were available at that time. Taking the seeds from raisins was a real messy business and as we sat round the table of an evening helping with the preparations, I can see father now, with a basin of hot water before him, extracting the seeds from the fruit and these promptly stuck to his fingers. He then had to place his fingers in the hot water in order to wash off the seeds. How many times, I wonder, did he have to do this while taking the seeds from a pound or two of fruit. Mother would be busy chopping suet and peeling and slicing apples, while we boys always volunteered for the job of cutting up the peel. There was method in our madness. The candied peel, oranges, lemons and limes came packed with a solid piece of sugar inside each half. This was removed before slicing the peel began, and while we sliced the peel, we also ate the sugar.

In my early days at school I would come home some weeks before Christmas to find the living room full of the smell of baking cakes and was greeted with, "Shut that door," as mother always believed that a sudden draught would mean that the cake would go down in the middle. Kitchen range ovens were not the easiest stoves to bake rich fruit cakes in, as it was always rather difficult to keep an even temperature. If there was insufficient heat the cake didn't bake properly, and the addition of extra fuel could always send the temperature too high and result in the cake burning. As the years went by she learned that one of the local bakers would bake Christmas cakes in their ovens, so that is where ours went after that. This meant that mother then got up earlier than usual to prepare the cakes on a Saturday morning, as this was the day the baker was prepared to do the job. A Sussex trug basket from the gardens had been scrubbed and cleaned the previous evening, and the tins containing the cake mixture were placed in it and the whole was covered with a clean tea cloth. It was then my job to take them to the baker's. They had to arrive before ten o'clock in the morning. The charge for baking a cake was threepence and I usually had to hand over sixpence to the cake baker as a tip in the hope that he would do a good job. He always seemed to, as the cakes were good. I used to go back to the bake-house any time after five in the afternoon to collect the cakes and carry them home. Perhaps ninepence seemed a lot in those times to bake a cake, but mother used to say it saved her that much in fuel, time and temper.

Fruit was another attraction at Christmas, as although we always had plenty of fruit at Beechwood there were the more exotic fruits which came from abroad and which we didn't normally have. A few days before the big event, father would go through the fruit room and take some of the better apples and pears out of store and from the grocer's or greengrocer's would come several kinds, oranges, bananas, boxes of dates and dried figs, and nuts of several kinds. I was never too bothered about the nuts, but managed my share of oranges and bananas. Nuts were father's favourites and strangely enough, out of all the different kinds of fruits he grew through the year, the only ones I remember him eating were apples.

At both school and Sunday School we were told the Christmas story. It always impressed upon us that the celebrations were first and foremost the birthday of Jesus. This repetition through our school days left its mark because even now we always start Christmas by attending the midnight service. At school, we sang carols, which gave us great enjoyment, and although I was no singer, I joined in with the rest.

Just before Christmas, father would look round the estate and cut or dig up a suitable Christmas tree. This was always large, seven feet or so high, and touched the sitting room ceiling when planted in a tea chest. Red crepe paper was used to cover the box. It was my job, after my brother had gone away to work, to decorate the tree. We had a really good selection of tree decorations, some of which looked quite expensive. I have no idea where they came from, as they were there from the time I can first remember, and I know that they were very carefully packed away in a big cardboard box after Christmas each year, stored in the large hanging cupboard in my parents' bedroom. We thought that when the tree was decorated it looked magnificent. We also had various streamers that went round the room, also stored carefully from year to year, and these always had to be kept out of the way of where the oil lamp stood because of the risk of fire.

Even after we knew there wasn't really a Father Christmas we still hung up a pillow case on Christmas Eve and this became the traditional way we received our presents. These consisted of one main present and the rest were odds and ends. Looking back I can recall four of the main presents I received in different years: a meccano set, a clockwork aeroplane with lights on the wings, a stamp album and a dynamo lighting set for my bicycle. The smaller things were: coloured pencils, sugar mice, sweets, drawing books, handkerchiefs, and I usually had a Rupert book because I loved the Rupert stories. These may not seem very much compared with what many children now receive, but they meant an awful lot to us and I never remember feeling disappointed or dissatisfied.

We always had a party or two and we looked forward to these very much. Bert, his sister and parents always came for an evening, and we in our turn went to his house. We also had other evenings when friends of my parents came and although they were all adults, I enjoyed these parties, perhaps because I was often the only child and got more attention than I normally did. Some years there would be a party up at the big house and these were always enjoyable. The adults usually went off into the drawing room where a whist drive was held, but the children ended up in the servants' hall where we had all sorts of party games with prizes all organised by some of the younger maids. The cook at Beechwood in my early days was quite an elderly lady whom I never liked very much. She was always very abrupt, and I was a bit frightened of her. One thing to do with her which sticks in my memory is the fact that on at least one occasion and probably twice, her son came to the party and sang, "Down, down, down among the dead men". What a choice for a Christmas party.

The Misses Barrington were strange ladies when it came to Christmas time. They joined with other gentry in having an area of the parish where they undertook to give Christmas presents to poorer people. They called at these houses and left either pot plants or groceries, and yet in the twenty-seven years my father worked for them, they never once gave my mother a Christmas present of any sort. Father always got the same, an extra ten shillings on his wages for the week before Christmas, and the children on the estate got something, but sometimes it was a peculiar gift for a child. I once got a small china dog. Up at the big house they were keen on jigsaw puzzles and did quite a lot in winter. Several times I was given one of those, more than once with pieces missing. I too, was quite fond of jigsaw puzzles, but it used to make me furious when I had put one together to find that a couple of pieces were no longer there.

One of the best things at Christmas was what was known as the school treat. It was called that, not because it came from the school, but because it was given to school children by the British Legion. This was held in the institute on a Saturday afternoon in early January before we went back to school at the beginning of the spring term. We used to gather there at about 3.30 p.m. and find long tables all laid for tea, which was served at 4 p.m. They always put on a good spread, with sandwiches of various sorts, plates of cakes and jelly and blancmange, with either orange juice or ginger beer to drink. I think the organisation was done by Mr Atkins whose presence ensured that we always behaved ourselves. After the tables were cleared away we all sat on chairs placed in rows and had some form of entertainment, perhaps a magician, conjuring or a puppet show. It was always great fun and the fact that we were all there together made it more enjoyable. When the show was over we were called up onto the stage by name, one at a time, to receive our gift. Mr Atkins was very good about this. He used to ask before the end of the autumn term what we would like, and did his best to see that we got something we wanted. One year I had a mathematical set comprising a pair of compasses, a pair of dividers, a protractor, set squares, pencil and ruler. In fact I have it still. When it was time to go home we put on hats and coats and as we left, various adults would be standing in the doorway and would give us small items such as an orange, a small bar of chocolate and a balloon to take with us. They were happy days.

CHAPTER NINE

On looking back, people kind and helpful, odd and drunk, come to mind, besides various incidents which caused a laugh or two in the village when they happened.

One of my favourite persons when I was a child, was Harry Loader who worked with my father at Beechwood, and with whom I spent many a happy hour. He was the sort of adult to whom you could talk. He would always listen and show interest in what you had to say, what you had been doing and what you hoped or wanted to do. He would talk to you about the work he was doing and explain why it had to be done. Never do I remember him telling me to clear off and leave him alone. When the jubilee celebrations took place in 1935 I told him the scouts were having a float of cowboys and Red Indians and I was to be a Red Indian brave. He immediately said, "Have you got your tomahawk?" and on my replying, "No," he said, "Come on, let's go and see what we can do," and off we went to a sort of workshop over the garage. There he found a piece of three-ply wood which he cut into the shape of a tomahawk blade and painted it with silver paint. He found a piece of wood suitable for a handle, which he cut a slot into in order to take the blade. He then bound the rest of the handle with strips of cloth which he painted green and orange. When all was dry a day or two later he fitted the blade to the handle and I had my tomahawk.

A similar thing happened at the time of the coronation

in 1937. When I told him we were having a float to represent a pirate ship, he immediately said, "Well, you'll want a cutlass, won't you?" Naturally I replied, "Oh, yes please." That was enough, off we went to the workshop, where he sketched out the shape of a cutlass on a tea chest lid, which he then cut out. It was then sandpapered down and thin cord was bound round the hilt to make it more comfortable to hold. He found a piece of tin which he fixed to make a hand guard and then the whole lot was painted silver. I was as pleased as could be with it and to me it looked quite realistic.

Harry was a member of the local fire brigade, all volunteers at the that time, and was telling me how they had been learning the fireman's lift, which enabled them to lift a person and place him over their shoulder and have a free hand for descending a ladder. We were in the stackyard at Beechwood at the time and I was pulling his leg and telling him I didn't think he could carry anyone down a ladder like that. He suddenly grabbed me, put his arm between my legs with his hand under my seat, and over his shoulder I went. He then carried me up a ladder and dumped me on top of a haystack. He had proved his point.

Harry, as a boy, had sung in the village choir, and it appears that once when he went to church he had been given a halfpenny to put in the collection, but he had spent it at the village sweet shop. On looking from the choir stalls towards the congregation, he had seen to his great surprise, that his father was seated there. He felt that when the collection bag came round he would have to put something in it because his father would be looking. Thinking quickly, he pulled a button from his cassock and dropped this into the bag. Unfortunately for Harry, the vicar was not pleased at finding a button among the collection coins and recognising it for what it was, decided to look at all the choir boys' cassocks. It was found that the only button that was missing was the one from Harry's cassock, so he was told that his services as a choir boy were no longer required. As he told me, this needed a lot of explaining to his father, but I was never told exactly what happened.

When I first knew Harry, he lived with his parents in a cottage on Acland Hill, and like half the cottages in the village at that time it had an outside bucket lavatory. Now Harry had always been a big eater, although he was as thin as a rake, and had been known to consume a complete rabbit at one meal. His father got a bit tired of the amount he managed to put away and said to him one day, "All you do boy is empty our larder and fill our shit house." There was a time when Miss Emma decided she would like to make some sloe gin and asked me whether I would get some sloes for her. I knew where a few blackthorn bushes grew, but they had only very few and small sloes on them at that time and they were of poor quality. I was stumped and really didn't know where I was going to get any worthwhile sloes from and for once father didn't seem able to help. I mentioned this problem to Harry who said straight away, "Meet me outside our cottage, after tea. Have your basket ready, we'll manage to find some sloes." I went off down Brook Lane and up Acland Hill and there was Harry waiting outside the cottage gate. We went on up the hill to a private estate called Rosemere where the lakes were. I had never been there before and as it was private we had no business to be on this land. This didn't seem to worry Harry very much, and as he was a local he knew jut what he was looking for and where they were to be found. Past the lakes and on northward towards the railway line we went until we came to some rough grazing ground and scattered here and there over this was a number of good blackthorns and better still they were well covered with sloes. Harry did most of the picking, too. He was a tall man and could reach the higher fruits and he really didn't want me getting in amongst the branches as blackthorns have some wickedly

157

sharp spikes which penetrate ordinary clothing. The sloes were duly delivered to Miss Emma who did not enquire where they came from. She must have been feeling in a benevolent mood as she rewarded me with half-a-crown (12½p). I felt a bit guilty about this and went to see Harry as I thought most of it really belonged to him. When I suggested this to him he grinned and said, "Keep it boy. They don't give much away. I doubt if you'll be as lucky again."

Harry had various sayings which I always found very funny as a child. If he knocked anything askew or over when moving towards a door he used to say, "Oh dear, we're departing in pieces," which obviously was a parody of the words "departing in peace" to be found in the bible and prayer book. On other occasions if he saw anyone loading a barrow which was standing behind them, and the person concerned kept turning round to fill it with leaves or manure or whatever it happened to be, there was usually a cry of, "Work with your arse behind you." One saying of his that really tickled me in those days and still brings a smile to my face was:

Father: "Piece more cake, Tommy?"
Tommy: "Yes, please, father."
Father: "What?"
Tommy: "No, thank you, father."
Father: "That's right. Speak up my boy."

I was talking to him once when I was quite young and I was telling him that someone at school had been calling me names, and he came out with, "Oh, I don't care what they call me, as long as it isn't late for dinner." After that remark my troubles didn't seem nearly so bad.

Eventually Harry left Beechwood and took over a greengrocer's shop in the village. In addition to the usual produce he sold pot plants from time to time. On meeting my father one day in the village, they had a chat and father was telling Harry what a good lot of cinerarias he had. Harry asked whether father had any to spare, thinking that he could dispose of some in his shop. In the end he had half a dozen or so and displayed them in the shop window. Of course, the inevitable happened. Miss Emma went up to the village and on her return sought out my father and told him, "Loader has got the most beautiful cinerarias in his shop this morning. Look, I have bought one." Father agreed that it was indeed, very good, and no doubt Harry had sold it to her without batting an eyelid. Little did she realise that she had just purchased one of her own pot plants.

There was a character in the village named Reg Iverson who lived at some out of the way place beyond the C.of E. mission room. He used to appear in the village from time to time, where he went the rounds of the pubs and got rather tipsy. One night, on his way home after having a drink at the local, father found Reg wandering about in the field of the Stag Hotel. He asked father whether he could put him on the right road for home, as he wasn't sure where he was. Father thought the easiest way was down through the fields to the lane by the river and from there Reg would be able to get up Dukes Hill. They walked together, well father walked and Reg rolled down to our cottage. Father then took Reg to the fence at the end of the garden hedge, saw him over it into Seven Acres and pointed out the way to the lane. Father saw him off, then went indoors. On the other side of Seven Acres the hedge that separated it from the beginning of Keith Rowland's land had at one time some gaps in it which had been filled by sections of iron fencing. These had been supported by chestnut posts which stuck up well above the fence. It seems that Reg, instead of going to the gate, had climbed a section of fencing and in attempting to get down the other side had slipped and one of the chestnut posts had gone up the back of his jacket and held him there with his feet above the ground. He managed to get his feet on to the iron rail, but being drunk he was unable to take off his jacket and spent the rest of the night unable to free himself. Father, on going out before six the next morning had glanced across Seven Acres and seen him there and had helped him out of his predicament. While doing this, father had roared with laughter, much to Reg's annoyance. Fortunately it was summer time and he seemed no worse for his experience. His late night, however, became an early morning. When they met after that, old Reg used to grin good-naturedly and say to father, "Your bloody fence."

I suppose in some ways father was a bit of a character too. He used to clip a certain number of graves for people who had relatives buried in the local churchyard. At times, if he had been busy, he would leave it until there was a bright moonlit night and then go off with his shears to clip these graves, and a sack to put the grass in. On emerging from the churchyard late one evening, he was greeted by a woman he knew quite well with, "Oh, Syd, I really don't know how you can go down there all on your own doing that work at night. I wouldn't dare." She in her turn got the answer, "Oh, you don't want to worry about that lot in there; they're harmless enough. It's the ones outside the gates you need to worry about."

One day in early spring when we were about twelve or so, Bert and I heard that there had been a haystack fire at the farm belonging to Matt Jardine, right on the extreme western boundary of the village. It must have been holiday time because we jumped on our bicycles and made our way to the farm to see what was going on. When we arrived there was certainly no blaze, but the firemen from Barnfield were still there shaking out hay, presumably to make sure there was none still smouldering. We watched for a while and then old Matt, who certainly was a character, appeared

160

from the farm house and called to the firemen in general, "Come on lads, fork it over and put as much black hay on the top as possible. Make it look bad, as the man from the insurance company is on his way, and I don't pay their bloody premiums for nothing. Make a good job of it and we'll split a barrel later." There was a bit of leg pulling, but I think most of the firemen were keen to help old Matt, or else they were looking forward to the contents of the barrel. One of the firemen shouted to Bert and me, "Do you want to come up on top and have a look?" We did, so we climbed the ladder and there they were with pitch forks picking up blackened hay and throwing it into the yard below. They looked some sketches with sooty faces and firemen's helmets tipped towards the back of their heads. Suddenly there was a cry from one corner of the stack, "Hell, it's still alight here." A fireman had moved some hay to reveal a red glow underneath. Another shouted across, "Hang on, that's just what I wanted." He then nipped across to where the hay was smouldering, knelt down, took a cigarette from a packet, put it in his mouth and bent over with the intention of lighting it from the uncovered patch of burning hay. The next moment we certainly got a laugh as the corner of the stack collapsed and as it fell away it was followed by the fireman who had been attempting to light his cigarette. It was like a scene from a Harry Tate play. It was then decided that Bert and I should leave before the insurance assessor arrived so we took the hint and returned home. What we didn't hear we couldn't talk about.

When I was writing about the London evacuees I stated that we knew what went on in the country. On reflection, the old farmer that hired the fields at Beechwood when I can first remember, was perhaps not too bright on all rural matters. He once found my brother's tortoise in Drive Field and on picking it up, the creature's head disappeared and the old man didn't seem to realise that it was an animal and thought it was just a shell. He thought the shell quite attractive so he took it home for his young daughter. Father saw him a few days later and asked him whether he had seen the tortoise. Then it dawned on him that that was what he had taken home. He hadn't bothered to look at it again after giving it to his daughter. Ted duly got his tortoise back.

Another villager I recall was old Dame Chandler, as she was known to all and sundry. She lived in a cottage near the middle of the village street. In the same house lived a younger man and his son. She always looked to me rather like a gypsy with her wrinkled brown face, earrings and long black skirt. She often was to be seen smoking a pipe. This was at the time when few women in the country smoked in public and certainly not out of doors. It was quite an attraction to children to see a woman with a pipe. I called to see her occasionally on my way back to school after dinner, as she bought rabbits' skins. When we had rabbit, the skin was saved, wrapped in newspaper and I took it to Dame Chandler, who, if my memory serves me correctly, paid twopence a skin. I know she always took the skin out of the paper and examined thoroughly before diving into her apron pocket for the coppers which she then handed over. She didn't like skins from rabbits that had been badly shot. What she did with the skins I don't know. She may have cured them herself in the garden behind the cottage, or she may have passed them on to someone else, but she obviously knew where she could dispose of them, and no doubt for more than she paid us.

I used to see the landlord of the Stag Hotel fairly regularly as I crossed his field four times a day. He was tall and slim and spoke very quickly with an American accent which he had acquired while living for some years in the United States. He used to use American colloquialisms which often I didn't understand. I recall his asking me where I was spending my vacation once, and I must admit that at that time I hadn't the faintest idea what he was talking about. While at The Stag he did a bit of advertising for custom by having some leaflets printed on which a verse he had written appeared. It ran as follows:

The ancients of old, drank water so cold,
And very soon withered away,
But the people round here, drink Dawson's beer
And flourish like flowers in May.

His wife, who was an American, took quite a liking to me and sometimes used to catch me on my way home from school in the afternoon. She would invite me into the hotel, then take me round to the dining room, which would be empty at that time of day. She then used to sit and chat to me while, apart from her, I sat in splendid isolation eating fruit salad and ice-cream, which was served by her daughter. She gave me a couple of encyclopaedias which I greatly cherished and which my daughter now has. Mr Dawson asked me on one occasion whether I knew that at one time a man had hanged himself in a lavatory at The Stag. I told him that I did know and he then said to me, "Never tell Mrs Dawson about it when talking to her. She would be scared to death if she knew about it and she just wouldn't stay here."

Another man in the village was one who, as boys we liked to imitate. Nicholas Arnold was a little, short fellow who always walked about in summer time without a jacket, but he wore a waistcoat and tucked his thumbs in the armholes. He also wore a flat cap tipped forward over his eyes. A lot of boys used to make fun of him, but I rather liked him and he was always pleasant to me and he also got on well with my father. Nevertheless we liked to put on a waistcoat and flat cap and pretend to be Nicholas Arnold. He got involved in an incident once, which nearly brought him to premature end. The landlord of the Stag Hotel at that time was a man called Ferris and he and Nicholas were in the field by the Stag tossing up clay pigeons and firing at them with twelve-bore shot guns. Nicholas wasn't doing very well and Ferris said to him, "Try my gun, Nicholas, you may have more success with a good quality gun." I don't know what Nicholas's gun was like, but I don't think he was short of money, as although he lived in quite a small house in the village street he never worked in all the years I remember him. Now, Ferris only ever used one barrel of his gun and kept a pull-through in the other but he failed to mention this, probably thinking that Nicholas knew, which he didn't. Nicholas Arnold took the gun from Ferris and inserted a couple of cartridges into it. He closed the barrel, up went a clay pigeon into the air, and he swung the gun round, aimed and fired. There was an almighty explosion and the barrel of the gun split from one end to the other. Nicholas, had of course, pulled the trigger which fired the cartridge in the barrel where the pull-through was stored. Strangely enough he wasn't injured at all, but he must have suffered one hell of a shock.

Some of the lads of the village got up to a few pranks from time to time. Maybe, for some, life got a bit monotonous in the village and these larks were a way of relieving high spirits. As far as I know, very little damage was ever done and certainly they were not vandals in the modern sense. The old farmer who took our tortoise was the subject of one laughable event. One evening, after his day's work, he put his old brown horse away in the stable, fed it, and then went off home. Imagine his surprise when he went for it next morning and found he had a completely white horse. Some of the lads had white-washed the old horse during the hours of darkness.

Keith Rowlands had beautiful yew hedges round his gardens at Southcourt and the iron gate which gave access to the path to the house door was locked at night. He got quite a shock, on looking out one morning, to observe a donkey doing its best to graze on his immaculate lawn. Some boys from the village had "borrowed" a donkey and taken it to Southcourt by night. They had also taken planks, one to be propped up against the outside of the hedge, one on the top, and the third sloping down onto the lawn the other side. The donkey had then been urged to make his way up the first plank, across the top of the hedge on the second and down the third on to the lawn of Southcourt. All the planks were then removed and returned to wherever they had come from. I did hear that Keith Rowlands, like Queen Victoria, was not amused. Even this prank was carried out when the lawn was hard and dry in summer, consequently no damage was caused.

Coming from the village towards Beechwood Drive gate, motorists observed a sign fixed to a post in the cricket field hedge which warned "Carriage Drive". On the other side of the road was another sign which read, "Golf Course". As mentioned earlier, the golf course entrance was opposite the drive gates of Beechwood, so once, on the night before a golf tournament someone saw fit to change the notices over. Although of course many of the golfers knew where the golf course was and probably never even noticed the signs had been altered, there were a few from away who made their way down to the house at Beechwood enquiring where the club house was.

One year, round about the 5th November, an incident involving fireworks took place. At the end of the lane which went past the Kings Head and the football field to the farmland beyond, stood a small cottage on the left hand side, under a walnut tree. The cottage was occupied by an elderly couple named Whiteside. A group of teenagers, including my brother, were in the football field lighting fireworks and throwing them towards the cottage. The resultant bangs were not appreciated by the old couple inside. After a few minutes and a few more explosions near his front door, the old man had had enough, so he came outside and in no uncertain terms remonstrated with the lads. While this was going on, unknown to Mr Whiteside, his wife had followed him outside. Sensing there was someone near, then hearing a movement he stretched out his arm in the darkness, grabbed the old lady and shouted triumphantly, "Got you." At this, the old lady, now rather frightened, screeched, "It's me." "Well," expostulated Mr Whiteside, "you silly old bugger. I might well have given you a thump under the bloody jaw." Any further remarks from either side were drowned by the hoots of laughter from the football field.

The vanishing parcel was a popular pastime for a limited period. A parcel, usually four bricks, was neatly wrapped in brown paper and tied with string. The parcel, which bore stamps and an address, would be placed on the grass verge beside the road. Attached to the parcel would be a length of green string which disappeared through the hedge to where the perpetrators of the joke would be in hiding. The first persons to be taken in by this ruse were Ted and Sarah Bowman. They would walk through the village daily from their farm near the Turnpike to the farm house in School Lane, with yokes across their shoulders and pails of milk suspended from the chains on either side. On seeing the parcel, Ted said to his sister, "Look, Sarah, there's a parcel. Pick it up." Sarah walked across to the parcel, bent over and just as she stretched out her hand to collect it, the parcel disappeared through the hedge bottom. Ted was a morose sort of character, and a stream of impolite language, starting, "Oh, so that's your bloody game," followed the parcel, much to the merriment of those in hiding. Several other villagers fell victim to this trick until the village constable came along and he, too, tried to pick up the parcel. As it disappeared, the policeman ran a few yards down the road, jumped over the gate, and was soon after the culprits. The boys ran across fields, through gardens, up and down alleys, still pursued by the law. The chase lasted for the best part of an hour, but in the end the boys scattered in different directions and the policeman failed to catch any of them. That was the end of the parcel game as although the lads had got away with it, they were all convinced that the local bobby knew who they were and to repeat it was just asking for trouble.

Outside the chapel in the High Street stood a notice board where posters or notices of forthcoming events were displayed. When nothing much was happening, the board bore biblical texts, or sometimes, as on this occasion, posters urging temperance and pointing out the evils of strong drink. When I went to school one morning, these had been taken down and the chapel notice board was advertising Page & Overton's beer and encouraging the villagers to drink Tamplin's brown ale, besides displaying a picture of Johnny Walker. Much could be done under the cover of darkness.

In similar vein was an escapade that involved the Stag Hotel. At the entrance to the private bar were wide, shallow steps which gradually narrowed as they neared the door. At the widest part stood two tubs, one on either side, containing rather nice conifer trees. Just across the street from The Stag was a grocer's shop and opposite the hotel entrance, a warehouse attached to the shop with a yard in front of it. This yard was often piled high with tea chests and other packing cases awaiting removal. One dark night they were removed, and morning revealed chests and cases outside the entrance to The Stag and opposite, neatly placed outside the doors of the warehouse were two conifer trees.

The village band were reputed on more than one occasion to have returned to the village in a worse state than they left. They went out playing on Christmas Eve and

New Year's Eve and sometimes ended up at Hulme's hop farm where the owner was known to make some pretty potent potato wine. They went in and played, and partook of wine, quite liberally it would seem, but all appeared well until they left the warmth of the farmhouse and got outside in the cold night air. The effects of the wine soon became obvious, not only from their playing but also from their gait. More than one bandsman fell headlong into the roadside ditch, I was told, as they staggered on their homeward way. Several instruments had, in due course, to be returned to the manufacturer's to have dents beaten out and I believe the tuba went back more than once. One follower of the band was reported to have been found on Christmas morning one year, asleep in a lorry behind the garage next to the cricket field gate, still wearing a blue suit, dark overcoat, white scarf and a bowler hat.

These amusing incidents were usually accepted by most folk with good humour, and all but the deadly serious, enjoyed a good laugh.

CHAPTER TEN

I left the village in 1942 when I joined the navy, and later I spent two and a half years in the east. The war was over when I returned to England in December 1945. We docked at Gourock late on a Friday evening and travelled up to a transit camp at Dunfermline, where we spent the night, but early the following morning I was on my way south to begin my leave. On arrival at the station in the next village to Barnfield, I had to wait a while for a taxi to transport me the three miles to my own village. The only car available was out, but when it returned I put my luggage in the boot and settled back to enjoy my first sight of the Sussex countryside for some time. As I gazed from the window as we approached the village, I saw, to my surprise, a man ploughing a field. Lots of ground around the village had been ploughed up for corn crops during wartime and there was nothing really surprising in the fact that the man was ploughing in December, but he was using a tractor to pull the plough. I had never previously seen a tractor in action on a farm in Barnfield.

On arrival at Beechwood, the taxi driver deposited me and my luggage on the wash outside the garage. As I made my way through the gardens to the cottage, they looked less tidy than usual, but obviously father had been short handed during the latter part of the war and he had had a job to cope. When I got to the cottage, after the greeting from my parents, we sat chatting for a while over a cup of tea, when mother suddenly said to me, "Oh, by the way, your dad has been talking to Miss Barrington. Their engine for the electric light is practically worn out, so they are going on the mains and what is more we're going to have electric light down here."

Tractors on the farms and electric light in the cottage and I'd only been back half an hour. No, things would never be the same again.

I didn't actually live in the village again, although I went home to visit my parents from time to time. After they departed I went even less, and now on my very infrequent visits to Barnfield, two songs, which John McCormack used to sing so beautifully, come to my mind. The first I think of is "The Old House" with its poignant words.

Lonely I wander through scenes of my childhood,
They call back to memory those happy days of yore.
Gone are the old folk, the house stands deserted,
No light in the windows, no welcome at the door.

Here's where the children played games on the heather,
Here's where they sailed their wee boats on the burn,
Where are they now? Some are dead, some have wandered,
No more to their homes shall those children return.

Lone is the house now and lonely the woodland,
The children are scattered, the old folk are gone,
Why stand I here like a ghost and a shadow,
'Tis time I was moving, 'tis time I passed on.

The other is "Oft in the Stilly Night", especially the first verse:

Oft in the stilly night,
Ere slumber's chain has bound me,
Fond memory brings the light
Of other days around me.
The smiles, the tears, of boyhood's years,
The words of love then spoken,
The eyes that shone, now dimmed and gone,
The cheerful hearts now broken.

I sometimes feel sad when I think back to the days that are no more. Things never were the same again.